Mystics of the Renaissance and their relation to modern thought

including Meister Eckhart, Tauler, Paracelsus, Jacob Boehme, Giordano Bruno, and others

Rudolf Steiner

translated by
Bertram Keightley

Alicia Editions

Contents

FOREWORD	1
INTRODUCTION	4
MEISTER ECKHART	21
THE FRIENDSHIP OF GOD (TAULER, SUSO AND RUYSBROECK)	31
CARDINAL NICHOLAS OF CUSA	48
AGRIPPA VON NETTESHEIM AND THEOPHRASTUS PARACELSUS	64
VALENTINE WEIGEL AND JACOB BOEHME	77
GIORDANO BRUNO AND ANGELUS SILESIUS	85
AFTERWORD	93

FOREWORD

The matter which I am laying before the public in this book formed the content of lectures which I delivered during last winter at the Theosophical Library in Berlin. I had been requested by Gräfin and Graf Brockdorff to speak upon Mysticism before an audience for whom the matters thus dealt with constitute a vital question of the utmost importance. Ten years earlier I could not have ventured to fulfil such a request. Not that the realm of ideas, to which I now give expression, did not even then live actively within me. For these ideas are already fully contained in my *Philosophy of Freedom* (Berlin, 1894. Emil Felber). But to give expression to this world of ideas in such wise as I do to-day, and to make it the basis of an exposition as is done on the following pages—to do this requires something quite other than merely to be immovably convinced of the intellectual truth of these ideas. It demands an intimate acquaintance with this realm of ideas, such as only many years of life can give. Only now, after having enjoyed that intimacy, do I venture to speak in such wise as will be found in this book.

Any one who does not approach my world of ideas without preconceptions is sure to discover therein contradiction after contradiction. I have quite recently (Berlin, 1900. S. Cronbach) dedicated a book upon the world conceptions of the nineteenth century to that great naturalist, Ernst Haeckel, and closed it with a defence of his thought-world. In the following expositions, I speak about the Mystics, from Master Eckhart to Angelus Silesius, with a full measure of devotion and acquiescence. Other "contradictions," which one critic or another may further count up against me, I shall not mention at all. It does not surprise me to be condemned from one side as a "Mystic" and from the other as a "Materialist." When I find that the Jesuit Father Müller has solved a difficult chemical problem, and I therefore in this particular matter agree with him unreservedly, one can hardly condemn me as an adherent of Jesuitism without being reckoned a fool by those who have insight.

Whoever goes his own road, as I do, must needs allow many a misunderstanding about himself to pass. That, however, he can put up with easily enough. For such misunderstandings are, in the main, inevitable in his eyes, when he recalls the mental type of those who misjudge him. I look back, not without humorous feelings, upon many a "critical" judgment that I have suffered in the course of my literary career. At the outset, matters went fairly well. I wrote about Goethe and his philosophy. What I said there appeared to many to be of such a nature that they could file it in their mental pigeon-holes. This they did by saying: "A work such as Rudolf Steiner's *Introduction to Goethe's Writings upon Natural Science* may, without hesitation, be described as the best that has been written upon this question."

When, later, I published an independent work, I had already grown a good bit more stupid. For now a well meaning critic offered the advice: "Before he goes on reforming further and gives his *Philosophy of Freedom* to the world, he should be pressingly advised first to work himself through to an understanding of these two philosophers [Hume and Kant]." The critic unfortunately knows only so much as he is himself able to read in Kant and Hume; practically, therefore, he simply advises me to learn to see no more in these thinkers than he himself sees. When I have attained that, he will be satisfied with me. Then when my *Philosophy and Freedom* appeared, I was found to be as much in need of correction as the most ignorant beginner. This I received from a gentleman who probably nothing else impelled to the writing of books except that he had not understood innumerable foreign ones. He gravely informs me that I should have noticed my mistakes if I had "made more thorough studies in psychology, logic, and the theory of knowledge"; and he enumerates forthwith the books I ought to read to become as wise as himself: "Mill, Sigwart, Wundt, Riehl, Paulsen, B. Erdmann."

What amused me especially was this advice from a man who was so "impressed" with the way he "understood" Kant that he could not even imagine how any man could have read Kant and yet judge otherwise than himself. He therefore indicates to me the exact chapters in question in Kant's writings from which I may be able to obtain an understanding of Kant as deep and as thorough as his own.

I have cited here a couple of typical criticisms of my world of ideas. Though in themselves unimportant, yet they seem to me to point, as symptoms, to facts which present themselves to-day as serious obstacles in the path of any one aiming at literary activity in regard to the higher problems of knowledge. Thus I must go on my way, indifferent, whether one man gives me the good advice to read Kant, or another hunts me as a heretic because I agree with Haeckel. And so I have also written upon Mysticism, wholly indifferent as to how a faithful and believing materialist may judge of me. I would only like—so that printers' ink may not be wasted wholly without need—to inform any one who may perchance advise me to read Haeckel's *Riddle of the Universe*, that during the last few months I have delivered about thirty lectures upon the said work.

I hope to have shown in this book that one may be a faithful adherent of the scientific conception of the world and yet be able to seek out those paths to the Soul along which Mysticism, rightly understood, leads. I even go further and say: Only he who knows the Spirit, in the sense of true Mysticism, can attain a full understanding of the facts of Nature. But one must not confuse true Mysticism with the "pseudo-mysticism" of ill-ordered minds. How Mysticism can err, I have shown in my *Philosophy of Freedom* (page 131 *et seq.*).

Dr. Rudolf Steiner

BERLIN, *September*, 1901.

INTRODUCTION

There are certain magical formulæ which operate throughout the centuries of Man's mental history in ever new ways. In Greece one such formula was regarded as an oracle of Apollo. It runs: "Know Thyself." Such sentences seem to conceal within them an unending life. One comes upon them when following the most diverse roads in mental life. The further one advances, the more one penetrates into the knowledge of things, the deeper appears the significance of these formulæ. In many a moment of our brooding and thinking, they flash out like lightning, illuminating our whole inner being. In such moments there quickens within us a feeling as if we heard the heart-beat of the evolution of mankind. How close do we not feel ourselves to personalities of the past, when the feeling comes over us, through one of their winged words, that they are revealing to us that they, too, had had such moments!

We feel ourselves then brought into intimate touch with these personalities. For instance, we learn to know Hegel intimately when, in the third volume of his *Lectures on the Philosophy of History* we come across the words: "Such stuff, one may say, the abstractions that we contemplate when we allow the philosophers to quarrel and battle in our study, and make it out to be thus or so—mere verbal abstractions! No! No! These are deeds of the world-spirit and therefore of destiny.

Therein the Philosophers are nearer to the Master than are those who feed themselves with the crumbs of the spirit; they read or write the Cabinet Orders in the original at once; they are constrained to write them out along with Him. The Philosophers are the Mystæ who, at the crisis in the inmost shrine, were there and took part." When Hegel said this, he had experienced one of those moments just spoken of. He uttered the phrases when, in the course of his remarks, he had reached the close of Greek philosophy; and through them he showed that once, like a gleam of lightning, the meaning of the Neoplatonic philosophy, of which he was just treating, had flashed upon him. In the instant of this flash, he had become intimate with minds like Plotinus and Proklus; and we become intimate with him when we read his words.

We become intimate, too, with that solitary thinker, the Pastor of Zschopau, M. Valentin Weigel, when we read the opening words of his little book *Know Thyself*, written in 1578: "We read in the wise men of old the useful saying, 'Know Thyself,' which, though it be right well used about worldly manners, as thus: 'regard well thyself, what thou art, seek in thine own bosom, judge thyself and lay no blame on others,' a saying, I repeat, which, though thus used of human life and manners, may well and appropriately be applied by us to the natural and supernatural knowing of the whole man; so indeed, that man shall not only consider himself and thereby remember how he should bear himself before people, but that he shall also know his own nature, inner and outer, in spirit and in Nature; whence he cometh and whereof he is made, to what end he is ordained." So, from points of view peculiar to himself, Valentin Weigel attained to insight which in his mind summed itself up in this oracle of Apollo.

A similar path to insight and a like relation to the saying "Know Thyself" may be ascribed to a series of deep-natured thinkers, beginning with Master Eckhart (1250-1327), and ending with Angelus Silesius (1624-1677), among whom may be found also Valentin Weigel himself.

All these thinkers have in common a strong sense of the fact that in man's knowing of himself there rises a sun which illuminates something very different from the mere accidental, separated personality of the beholder. What Spinoza became conscious of in the ethereal heights of pure thought,—*viz.*, that "the human soul possesses an adequate knowledge of the Eternal and Infinite Being of God,"—that same consciousness lived in them as immediate feeling; and self-knowledge was to them the path leading to this Eternal and Infinite Being. It was clear to them that self-knowledge in its true form enriched man with a new sense, which unlocked for him a world standing in relation to the world accessible to him without this new sense as does the world of one possessing physical sight to that of a blind man.

It would be difficult to find a better description of the import of this new sense than the one given by J. G. Fichte in his Berlin Lectures (1813):

"Imagine a world of men born blind, to whom all objects and their relations are known only through the sense of touch. Go amongst them and speak to them of colours and other relations, which are rendered visible only through light. Either you are talking to them of nothing,—and if they say this, it is the luckier, for thus you will soon see your mistake, and, if you cannot open their eyes, cease your useless talking,—or, for some reason or other, they *will* insist upon giving some meaning or other to what you say; then they can only interpret it in relation to what they know by touch. They will seek to feel, they will imagine they do feel light and colour, and the other incidents of visibility, they will invent something for themselves, deceive themselves with something within the world of touch, which they will call colour. Then they will misunderstand, distort, and misinterpret it."

The same thing applies to what the thinkers we are speaking of sought after. They beheld a new sense opening in self-knowledge, and this sense yielded, according to their experiences, views of things which are simply non-existent for one who does not see in self-knowledge what distinguishes it from all other kinds of knowing. One in whom this new sense has not been opened, believes that self-knowing, or self-perception, is the same thing as perception through the outer senses, or through any other means acting from without. He thinks: "Knowing is knowing, perceiving is perceiving." Only in the one case the object is something lying in the world outside, in the other this object is his own soul. He finds words merely, or at best, abstract thoughts, in that which for those who see more deeply is the very foundation of their inner life; namely, in the proposition: that in every other kind of knowing or perception we have the object perceived outside of ourselves, while in self-knowledge or self-perception we stand within that object; that we see every other object coming to us already complete and finished off, while in ourselves we, as actors and creators, are weaving that which we observe within us. This may appear to be nothing but a merely verbal explanation, perhaps even a triviality; it may appear, on the other hand, as a higher light which illuminates every other cognition. One to whom it appears in the first way, is in the position of a blind man, to whom one says: there is a glittering object. He hears the words, but for him the glitter is not there. He might unite in himself the whole sum of knowledge of his time; but if he does not feel and realise the significance of self-knowledge, then it is all, in the higher sense, a blind knowledge.

The world, outside of and independent of us, exists for us by communicating itself to our consciousness. What is thus made known must needs be expressed in the language peculiar to ourselves. A book, the contents of which were offered in a language unknown to us, would for us be without meaning. Similarly, the world would be meaningless for us did it not speak to us in our own tongue; and the same language which reaches us from things, we also hear from within ourselves. But in that case, it is we ourselves who speak. The really important point is that we should correctly apprehend the transposition which occurs when we close our perception against external things and listen only to that which then speaks from within. But to do this needs this new sense. If it has not been awakened, we believe that in what is thus told us about ourselves we are hearing only about something external to us; we fancy that somewhere there is hidden something which is speaking to us in the same way as external things speak. But if we possess this new sense, then we know that these perceptions differ essentially from those relating to external things. Then we realise that this new sense does not leave what it perceives outside of itself, as the eye leaves the object it sees; but that it can take up its object wholly into itself, leaving no remainder. If I see a thing, that thing remains outside of me; if I perceive myself, then I myself enter into my perception. Whoever seeks for something more of himself than what is perceived, shows thereby that for him the real content in the perception has not come to light. Johannes Tauler (1300-1361), has expressed this truth in the apt words: "If I were a king and knew it not, then should I be no king. If I do not shine forth for myself in my own self-perception, then for myself I do not exist. But if for myself I do shine out, then I possess myself also in my perception, in my own most deeply original being. There remains no residue of myself left outside of my perception."

J. G. Fichte, in the following words, vigorously points to the difference between self-perception and every other kind of perception: "The majority of men could be more easily brought to believe themselves a lump of lava in the moon than an 'ego.' Whoever is not at one with himself as to this, understands no thorough-going philosophy and has need of none. Nature, whose machine he is, will guide him in all the things he has to do without any sort of added help from him. For philosophising, self-reliance is needed, and this one can only give to oneself. We ought not to want to see without the eye; but also we ought not to maintain that it is the eye which sees."

Thus the perception of oneself is also the awakening of oneself. In our cognition we combine the being of things with our own being. The communications, which things make to us in our own language, become members of our own selves. An object in front of me is not separated from me, once I have known it. What I am able to receive from it becomes part and parcel of my own being. If, now, I awaken my own self, if I become aware of the content of my own inner being, then I also awaken to a higher mode of being, that which from without I have made part of my own being. The light that falls upon me at my awakening falls also upon whatever I have made my own from the things of the outside world. A light springs up within me and illumines me, and with me all that I have cognised of the world. Whatever I might know would remain blind knowledge, did not this light fall upon it. I might search the world through and through with my perception; still the world would not be that which in me it must become, unless that perception were awakened in me to a higher mode of being.

That which I add to things through this awakening is not a new idea, is not an enrichment of the content of my knowing; it is an uplifting of the knowledge, of the cognition, to a higher level, where everything is suffused with a new glory. So long as I do not raise my consciousness to this level, all knowledge continues to be for me, in the higher sense, valueless. The things are there without my presence. They have their being in themselves. What possible meaning could there be in my linking with their being, which they have outside and apart from me, another spiritual existence in addition, which repeats the things over again within me? If only a mere repetition of things were involved, it would be senseless to carry it out. But, really, a mere repetition is only involved so long as I have not awakened, along with my own self, the mental content of these things upon a higher level. When this occurs, then I have not merely repeated within myself the being of things, but I have brought it to a new birth on a higher level. With the awakening of my self, there is accomplished a spiritual re-birth of the things of the world.

What the things reveal in this re-birth did not previously belong to them. There, without, stands the tree. I take it up into my consciousness. I throw my inner light upon that which I have thus conceived. The tree becomes in me more than it is outside. That in it which finds entrance through the gate of the senses is taken up into a conscious content. An ideal replica of the tree is within me, and that has infinitely more to say about the tree than what the tree itself, outside, can tell me. Then, for the first time there shines out from within me, towards the tree, what the tree is. The tree is now no longer the isolated being that it is out there in space. It becomes a link in the entire conscious world that lives in me. It links its content with other ideas that are in me. It becomes a member of the whole world of ideas that embraces the vegetable kingdom; it takes its place, further, in the series of all that lives.

Another example: I throw a stone in a horizontal direction away from me. It moves in a curved line and after some time falls to the ground. I see it in successive moments of time in different places. Through observation and reflection I acquire the following: During its motion the stone is subject to different influences. If it were subject only to the influence of the impulse which I imparted to it, it would go on flying for ever in a straight line, without altering its velocity. But now the earth exerts an influence upon it. It attracts the stone towards itself. If, instead of throwing the stone, I had simply let it go, it would have fallen vertically to earth; and its velocity in doing so would have constantly increased. From the mutual interaction of these two influences arises that which I actually see.

Let us assume that I could not in thought separate the two influences, and from this orderly combination put together again in thought what I see: in that case, the matter would end with the actual happening. It would be mentally a blind staring at what happened; a perception of the successive positions which the stone occupies. But in actual fact, matters do *not* stop there. The whole occurrence takes place twice. Once outside, and then my eye sees it; then my mind causes the whole happening to repeat itself again, in a mental or conscious manner. My inner sense must be directed upon the mental occurrence, which my eye does not see, and then it becomes clear to that sense that I, by my own inner power, awaken that occurrence as a mental one.

Again, another sentence of J. G. Fichte's may be quoted which brings this fact clearly before the mind. "Thus the new sense is the sense for the spirit; that for which there exists only spirit and absolutely nothing else, and for which also the 'other,' the given being, assumes the form of spirit and transforms itself into spirit, for which therefore *being* in its own proper form has actually disappeared. . . . There has been the faculty of seeing with this sense ever since men have existed, and all that is great and excellent in the world, which alone upholds humanity, originates in what has been seen by means of this sense. It is, however, not the case that this sense has been perceived or known in its difference and its contrast with that other, ordinary sense. The impressions of the two senses melted into one another, life fell apart into these two halves without a bond of union."

The bond of union is created by the fact that the inner sense grasps in its spirituality the spiritual element which it awakens in its intercourse with the outer world. That which we take up into our consciousness from outside things thereby ceases to appear as a mere meaningless repetition. It appears as something new over against that which only external perception can give. The simple occurrence of throwing the stone, and my perception thereof, appear in a higher light when I make clear to myself the kind of task which my inner sense has to perform in regard to the whole thing. In order to fit together in thought the two influences and their modes of action, an amount of mental content is needed which I must already have acquired when I cognise the flying stone. I therefore apply a spiritual content already stored up within me to something that confronts me in the external world. And this occurrence in the external world fits itself into the spiritual content already present. It reveals itself in its own special individuality as an expression of this content.

Through the understanding of my inner sense, there is thus disclosed to me the nature of the relation that obtains between the content of this sense and the things of the external world. Fichte would say that without the understanding of this sense, the world falls apart for me into two halves: into things outside of me, and into pictures of these things within me. The two halves become united when the inner self understands itself and consequently recognises clearly what sort of illumination it throws upon things in the cognitive process. And Fichte could also venture to say that this inner sense sees only Spirit. For it perceives how the Spirit enlightens the sense-world by making it part and parcel of the spiritual world. The inner sense causes the outer sense-world to arise within itself as a spiritual being on a higher level. An external object is completely known when there is no part of it which has not thus undergone a spiritual re-birth. Thus every external object fits itself into a spiritual content, which, when it has been grasped by the inner sense, shares the destiny of self-knowledge. The spiritual content, which belongs to an object through its illumination from within, merges itself wholly, like the very self, into the world of ideas, leaving no remainder behind.

These developments contain nothing which is susceptible or even in need of logical proof. They are nothing but the results of inner experience. Whoever calls into question this content, shows only that he is lacking in this inner experience. It is impossible to dispute with him; as little could one discuss colour with a blind man.

It must not, however, be contended that this inner experience is made possible only through the special endowment of a few chosen people. It is a common property. Every one can enter upon the path to this experience who does not of his own will shut himself against it. This closing up of oneself against it, is, however, common enough. And in dealing with objections raised in this direction, one always has the feeling that it is not so much a matter of people being unable to attain this inner experience, as of their having hopelessly blocked the entrance to it with all kinds of logical spiders' webs. It is almost as if some one looking through a telescope and discovering a new planet should yet deny its existence because his calculations have shown that there can be no planet in that position.

But with all this there is still in most people the clearly marked feeling that all that really lies in the being of things cannot be completely given in what the outer senses and the analysing understanding can cognise. They then believe that the remainder so left over must be just as much in the external world as are the things of our perceptions themselves. They think that there must be something which remains unknown to cognition. What they ought to attain by again perceiving with the inner sense, on a higher plane, the very object which they have already cognised and grasped with the understanding,—this they transfer as something inaccessible and unknown into the external world. Then they talk of the limits of knowledge which prevent our reaching the "thing-in-itself." They talk of the unknown "being" of things. That this very "being" of things shines out when the inner sense lets its light fall upon the things, is what they will not recognise. The famous "Ignorabimus" speech of the scientist, Du Bois-Reymond, in the year 1876, furnished a particularly blatant example of this error. We are supposed to be able to get in every direction only so far as to be able to see in all natural processes the manifestations of "matter." What "matter" itself is, we are supposed to be unable to know. Du Bois-Reymond contends that we shall never succeed in penetrating to wherever it is that "matter" leads its ghostly life in space. The reason why we cannot get there lies, however, in the fact that there is nothing whatsoever to be looked for there. Whoever speaks like Du Bois-Reymond must have a feeling that the knowledge of Nature yields results which point to a something further and other which Nature-knowledge itself cannot give. But he refuses to follow the road,—the road of inner experience, which leads to this other. Therefore he stands at a complete loss before the question of "matter" as before a dark riddle. In him who treads the path of inner experience, objects attain to a new birth; and that in them which remains unknown to outer experience then shines forth.

In such wise the inner being of man obtains light not only as regards itself but also as regards external things. From this point of view an endless perspective opens out before man's knowledge. Within him shines a light whose illumination is not restricted to that which is within him. It is a sun which lights up all reality at once. Something makes its appearance in us which links us with the whole world. No longer are we simply isolated, chance human beings, no longer this or that individual. The entire world reveals itself in us. It unveils to us its own coherence; and it unveils to us how we ourselves as individuals are bound up with it. From out of self-knowledge is born knowledge of the world. And our own limited individuality merges itself spiritually into the great interconnected world-whole, because in us something has come to life that reaches out beyond this individuality, that embraces along with it everything of which this individuality forms a part.

Thinking which does not block up its own road to inner experience with logical preconceptions always comes, in the long run, to a recognition of the entity that rules in us and connects us with the entire world, because through this entity we overcome the opposition of "inner" and "outer" in regard to man. Paul Asmus, the keen-sighted philosopher, who died young, expressed himself as follows about this position (*cp.* his book *Das Ich und das Ding an Sich*, p. 14 *et seq.*):—"Let us make it clear by an example: imagine a piece of sugar; it is square, sweet, impenetrable, etc., etc., these are one and all qualities which we understand; one thing, however, hovers before us as something totally different, that we do not understand, that is so different from ourselves that we cannot penetrate into it without losing ourselves; from the mere surface of which thought starts back afraid. This one thing is the unknown bearer of all these qualities; the thing-in-itself, which constitutes the inmost self of the object. Thus Hegel rightly says that the entire content of our perception is related as mere accident to this obscure subject, while we, without penetrating into its depths, merely attach determinations to what it is in itself,—which ultimately, since we do not know the thing itself, remain merely subjective and have no objective value. Conceptual thought, on the other hand, has no such unknowable subject, whose determinations might be mere accidents, but the objective subject falls within the concept. If I cognise anything, then it is present in its entire fulness in my conception; I am at home in the inmost shrine of its being, not because it has no proper being-in-itself of its own, but because it compels me to re-think its concept, in virtue of that necessity of the concept which hovers over us both and appears subjectively in me and objectively in the concept itself. Through this re-thinking there reveals itself to us at the same time, as Hegel says,—just as this is our own subjective activity—the true nature of the object." So can speak only a man who is able to illuminate the life of thought with the light of inner experience.

In my *Philosophy of Freedom* (Berlin, 1894, Verlag Emil Felber), starting from other points of view, I have also pointed out the root-fact of the inner life (p. 46): "It is therefore unquestionable: in our thinking we hold the world-process by one corner, where we must be present, if it is to come about at all. And that is just the very thing we are here concerned with. That is just the reason why things seem to confront me so mysteriously: that I am so without any share in their coming into existence. I simply find them there; in thinking, however, I know how it is done. Hence one can find no more original starting point for a consideration of the world-process than that of thought."

For one who looks thus upon the inner life of man, it is also obvious what is the meaning of human cognition within the whole world-process. It is not a mere empty accompaniment to the rest of the world happenings. It would be such if it represented merely an ideal repetition of what is outwardly present. But in cognition something is accomplished which accomplishes itself nowhere in the outer world: the world-process sets before itself its own spiritual being. The world-process would be to all eternity a mere half-thing, if it did not attain to this confrontation. Therewithal man's inner experience finds its place in the objective world-process; and without it that process would be incomplete.

It is apparent that only the life which is ruled by the inner sense, man's highest spiritual life in its most proper sense,—it is this life only which can thus raise man above himself. For only in this life does the being of things unveil itself before itself. The matter lies quite differently in regard to the lower perceptive power. For instance, the eye which meditates the seeing of an object is the theatre of a process which, in contrast to the inner life, is exactly like any other external process. My organs are members of the spacial world like other things, and their perceptions are processes in time like any others. Further, their being only appears when they are sunk into the inner life. I thus live a double life; the life of an object among other objects, which lives within its own embodiment and perceives through its organs what lies outside this embodiment; and above this life a higher life, that knows no such inside and outside, that extends, stretching and bridging over both the outside world and itself. I shall therefore be forced to say: at one time I am an individual, a limited "self"; at another time I am a general, universal "Self." This, too, Paul Asmus has expressed in excellent words (*cp.* his book: *Die indogermanischen Religionen in den Hauptpunkten ihrer Entwickelung*, p. 29 of Vol. I.):

"The activity of merging ourselves in something else, is what we call 'thinking'; in thinking, the ego has fulfilled its concept, it has given itself up as a single thing; therefore, in thinking do we find ourselves in a sphere which is alike for all, for the principle of separateness which is involved in the relation of our 'self' to that which is other than itself has vanished in the activity of the self-cancelling of the single 'self,' and there remains then only the 'Self-hood' common to all."

Spinoza has exactly the same thing in view when he describes, as the highest activity of knowing, that which "advances from an adequate conception of the real nature of some of the attributes of God to an adequate knowledge of the nature of things." This advancing is no other than the illumination of things with the light of inner experience. Spinoza describes in glowing colours the life in this inner experience: "The highest virtue of the soul is to know God, or to obtain insight into things in the third—the highest—mode of knowing. This virtue is the greater, the more the soul knows things by this method of knowing; thus he who can grasp things in this mode of knowing attains the highest human perfection and consequently becomes filled with the highest joy, accompanied, moreover, by the conceptions of himself and of virtue. Thus there arises from this mode of knowing the highest peace of soul that is possible."

He who knows things in this way, transforms himself within himself; for his single separated "self" becomes at such moments absorbed by the universal "Self"; all beings appear not to a single limited individual in subordinated importance, they appear to "themselves." On this level there remains no difference between Plato and me; what separated us belongs to a lower level of cognition. We are separated only as individuals; the individual which works within us is one and the same. But about this fact it is impossible to argue with one who has no experience of it. He will everlastingly emphasise: Plato and you are two. That this duality, that all multiplicity, is reborn as unity in the outbursting life of the highest level of knowledge: that cannot be proved, that must be experienced. Paradoxical as it may sound, it is the truth: the idea which Plato conceived and the like idea which I conceive are not two ideas. It is one and the same idea. And there are not two ideas: one in Plato's head and one in mine; but in the higher sense Plato's head and mine interpenetrate each other; all heads interpenetrate which grasp one and the same idea; and this idea is only once there as a single idea. It is there; and the heads all go to one and the same place in order to have this idea in them.

The transformation that is brought about in the whole being of man when he learns to see things thus, is indicated in beautiful words by the Hindu poem, the Bhagavad-Gîtâ, about which Wilhelm von

Humboldt said that he was thankful to the fate which had allowed him to live long enough to become acquainted with this work. In this poem, the inner light declares: "An eternal ray from myself, having attained a distinct existence in the world of personal life, draws around itself the five senses and the individual soul, which belong to nature. When the spirit, shining from above, embodies itself in space and time, or when it quits embodiment, it seizes upon things and carries them away with it, as the zephyr seizes the perfumes of the flowers and bears them away with it. The inner light rules the ear, touch, taste and smell, as also the emotions: it knits together the link between itself and the objects of the senses. The ignorant know not when the inner light shines forth or is extinguished, nor when it is married to objects; only he who partakes of the inner light can know thereof."

So strongly does the Bhagavad-Gîtâ insist upon the transformation of the man, that it says of the wise man that he can no longer err, no longer sin. If, apparently, he errs or sins, then he must illuminate his thoughts or his actions with a light wherein that no longer appears as error or as sin which to the ordinary consciousness appears as such. "He who has raised himself and whose knowledge is of the purest kind, he kills not, nor does he stain himself, even though he should have slain another." This points only to the same basic mood of the soul flowing from the highest knowledge, of which Spinoza, after having described it in his *Ethics*, breaks out into the passionate words: "Here is concluded that which I aimed to bring forward in regard to the power of the soul over its affections or in regard to the freedom of the soul. Hence it is clear how very greatly the wise man is superior to the ignorant, and how much more powerful than he who is ruled only by his lusts. For the ignorant is not merely driven hither and thither by external causes in many ways and never attains to the true peace of soul, but he also lives in ignorance of himself, of God and of things, and when his suffering ceases, his existence ceases also; while on the other hand, the wise man, as such, feels hardly any disturbance in his spirit and ever enjoys the true peace of the soul. Even if the road which I have outlined as leading thereto appears very difficult, still it can be found. And well may it be difficult, because it is so seldom found. For how could it be possible, if salvation lay close at hand and could be found without great trouble, that it should be neglected by almost all? Yet all that is noble is as difficult as it is rare."

Goethe has indicated in monumental form the point of view of the highest knowledge in the words: "If I know my relation to myself and to the outer world, I call it truth. And thus every one can have his own truth, and yet it is always one and the same." Each has his own truth: because each is an individual, separate being, beside and along with others. These other beings act upon him through his organs. From the individual standpoint at which he is placed, and according to the constitution of his power of perception, he builds up his own truth for himself in intercourse with the things around him. He acquires his relation to things. If, then, he enters into self-knowledge, if he learns to know his relation to himself, then his special separate truth is merged in the universal Truth; and this universal Truth is in all the same.

The understanding of the raising of the individual, of the single self, into the Universal Self in the personality, is regarded by deeper natures as the secret which reveals itself in the inmost heart of man as the root-mystery of life. And Goethe has found an apt expression for this: "And so long as thou hast not that, this: Die and Become! Then thou art but a melancholy guest upon this dark earth."

Not a mere repetition in thought, but a real part of the world-process, is that which goes on in man's inner life. The world would not be what it is if the factor belonging thereto in the human soul did not play its part. And if one calls the highest which is attainable by man the Divine, then one must say that this Divine is not present as something external, to be repeated pictorially in the human mind, but that this Divine is awakened in man. Angelus Silesius has found the right words for this: "I know that without me God can live no instant; if I become nothing, He must of necessity give up the ghost." "Without me God may make no single smallest worm: if I do not sustain it with Him, then it must straightway perish." Only he can make such an assertion who presupposes that in man something comes to light, without which external being cannot exist. If everything pertaining to the "worm" were there present without man, then one could not possibly say that it must perish if man did not sustain it.

The innermost kernel of the world comes to life as spiritual content in self-knowledge. The experience of self-knowledge means for man working and weaving within the kernel of the world. He who is permeated with self-knowledge naturally carries out his own action in the light of self-knowledge. Human action is—in general—determined by motives. Robert Hamerling, the poet-philosopher, has rightly said (*Atomistik des Willens*, p. 213):

"A man can indeed do what he wills—but he cannot will whatever he pleases, because his will is determined by motives. He cannot will whatever he pleases? Look again at these words more closely. Is there any sensible meaning in them? Freedom of the will ought then to consist in being able to will something without reason, without motive. But what does willing mean other than the 'having a reason' for preferring to do or endeavour to attain this, rather than that? To will something without reason, without motive, would mean to will something 'without willing it.' The concept of motive is inseparably bound up with that of willing. Without a definite motive the will is an empty potentiality: only through a motive does it become active and real. It is therefore quite correct that man's will is in so far not free as its direction is always determined by the strongest motive."

For all action that is not accomplished in the light of self-knowledge, the motive, the reason for action, must needs be felt as a constraint. But the matter is otherwise when the reason or motive is taken up into self-knowledge. Then this reason becomes a part of the self. The willing is no longer determined; it determines itself. The law-abidingness, the motives of willing, now no longer rule over the one who wills, but are one and the same with this willing. To illuminate the laws of one's action with the light of self-observation means to overcome all constraint of motive. By so doing, will transfers itself into the realm of freedom.

It is not all human action which bears the marks of freedom. Only such action is free action which in its every part is lighted up with the glow of self-observation. And because self-observation raises the individual self up to the Universal Self, therefore free action is that which flows from the Universal Self. The old controversy whether man's will is free or subject to a universal law, to an unalterable necessity, is a problem wrongly stated. All action is bound which is done by a man as an individual; all action free which is accomplished after his spiritual re-birth. Man, therefore, is not, in general, either free or bound. He is both the one and the other. He is bound before his re-birth; and he can become free through this re-birth. The individual upward development of man consists in the transformation of unfree willing into will possessing the character of freedom. The man who has realised the law-abidingness of his action as his own, has overcome the constraint of this law-abidingness and therewith of un-freedom. Freedom is not from the outset a fact of human existence, but a goal thereof.

With the attainment of free action, man resolves a contradiction between the world and himself. His own deeds become deeds of universal being. He feels himself in the fullest harmony with this universal being. He feels every discord between himself and another as the outcome of a not yet fully awakened self. But such is the fate of the self, that only in its separation from the whole can it find its contact with this whole. Man would not be man if he were not shut off as an individual self from everything else; but also he is not man in the highest sense if he does not, as such a shut-off and isolated self, widen himself out again into the Universal Self. It belongs through and through to the nature of man that it should overcome an inherent contradiction which has lain therein from the beginning.

Any one who regards spirit as, in the main, logical understanding, may well feel his blood run cold at the idea that objects should be supposed to undergo their re-birth in spirit. He will compare the fresh, living flower, outside there in its fulness of colour, with the cold, faded, schematic thought of the flower. He will feel himself particularly ill at ease with the conception that the man who draws his motives from the solitude of his own self-consciousness is more free than the original, naïve personality which acts from its immediate impulses, from the fulness of its own nature. To one who sees only one-sided logic, another man who sinks himself into his own inner being will appear like a mere walking scheme of concepts, like a mere ghost in contrast with the man who remains in his own natural individuality.

Such objections to the re-birth of things in spirit are especially to be heard from those whose power of perception fails in the presence of things with a purely spiritual content; although they are well provided with healthy organs of sense-perception and with impulses and passions full of life. As soon as they are called upon to perceive the purely spiritual, the power to do so fails them; they can deal only with mere conceptual husks, when even they are not limited to empty words. They remain, therefore, in what concerns spiritual content, men of "dry, abstract understanding." But the man who in things purely spiritual possesses a gift of perception like that in things of the senses, finds life assuredly not the poorer when he has enriched it with its spiritual content. If I look out upon a flower, why should its rich colours lose aught whatever of their freshness, because not only does my eye see the colours, but my inner sense also perceives the spiritual being of the flower? Why should the life of my personality become poorer, because I do not follow my passions and impulses in spiritual blindness, but illuminate them throughout with the light of higher knowledge? Not poorer, but fuller, richer, is that life which is given back again in the spirit.

MEISTER ECKHART

The world of Meister Eckhart's conceptions is aglow through and through with the feeling that things become reborn as higher entities in the spirit of man. Like the greatest Christian theologian of the Middle Ages, St. Thomas Aquinas, who lived from 1225 till 1274, Meister Eckhart belonged to the Dominican Order. Eckhart was an unqualified admirer of St. Thomas; and this will seem the more intelligible when we fix our gaze upon Eckhart's whole manner of conceiving things. He believed himself to be as completely in harmony with the teachings of the Christian Church as he assumed a like agreement on the part of St. Thomas. Eckhart had neither the desire to take aught away from the content of Christianity, nor the wish to add anything to it; but he desired to bring forward this content anew in his own way. It forms no part of the spiritual needs of a personality such as he was to set up new truths of this or the other kind in the place of old ones. Such a personality has grown completely intertwined with the content which it has received from tradition; but it craves to give to this content a new form, a new life.

Eckhart desired, without doubt, to remain an orthodox Christian. The Christian truths were his own; only he desired to regard these truths in another way from that, for instance, in which St. Thomas Aquinas had done. St. Thomas accepted two sources of knowledge: Revelation, in matters of faith, and Reason, in those of research. Reason recognises the laws of things, that is, the spiritual in nature. Reason can raise itself above nature and grasp in the spirit from one side the Divine Being underlying nature. But it does not attain in this way to merging itself in the full being of God. A still higher truth-content must come to meet it. That is given in the Holy Scripture, which reveals what man cannot attain to through himself. The truth-content of the Scripture must be accepted by man; Reason can defend it, Reason can seek to understand it as well as possible through its powers of knowing; but never can Reason engender that truth from within the spirit of man. Not what the spirit perceives is the highest truth, but what has come to this spirit from without.

St. Augustine declares himself unable to find within himself the source for that which he should believe. He says: "I would not believe in the Gospel, did not the authority of the Catholic Church move me thereto." That is in the same spirit as the Evangelist, who points to the external testimony: "That . . . which we have heard, which we have seen with our eyes, which we have looked upon, and our hands have handled, of the Word of Life; . . . that which we have seen and heard declare we unto you, that ye also may have fellowship with us." But Meister Eckhart would rather impress upon man the words of Christ: "It is expedient for you that I go away: for if I go not away, the Comforter will not come unto you"; and he explains these words by saying: "Just as if he had said: Ye have set too much joy upon my present appearance, therefore the full joy of the Holy Ghost cannot come to you."

Eckhart thinks that he is speaking of no God other than that God of whom Augustine, and the Evangelist, and Thomas, speak, and yet this testimony as to God is not his testimony, their witness is not his. "Some people want to see God with the same eyes they see a cow withal, and want to love God as they would love a cow. So they love God for the sake of outer riches and inner comfort; but such folk do not rightly love God. . . . Simple folk fancy they should behold God as though He stood there and they here. But it is not so. God and I are one in the act of knowing (*im Erkennen*)." What underlies such expressions in Eckhart's mouth is nothing else than the experience of the inner sense; and this experience shows him things in a higher light. He therefore believes himself to have no need of an external light in order to attain to the highest insight: "A Master says: God became man, whereby the whole human race is uplifted and made worthy. Thereof may we be glad that

Christ our brother of His own strength rose above all the choirs of angels and sitteth at the right hand of the Father. That Master spake well; but, in truth, I would give little for it. What would it help me, had I a brother who was a rich man, and I therewithal a poor man? What would it help me, had I a brother who was a wise man, and I were a fool?. . . The Heavenly Father begetteth His Only-Begotten Son in Himself and in me. Wherefore in Himself and in me? I am one with Him; and He has no power to shut me out. In the self-same work, the Holy Ghost receives its being and proceeds from me, as from God. Wherefore? I am in God, and if the Holy Ghost takes not its being from me, neither does it take it from God. In no wise am I shut out."

When Eckhart recalls the saying of St. Paul: "Put ye on Jesus Christ," he means to imply in this saying the meaning: Sink yourselves into yourselves, dive down into self-contemplation: and from out the depths of your being, God will shine forth to meet you; He illumines all things for you; you have found Him within you; you have become united with God's Being. "God became man, that I might become God."

In his booklet upon *Loneliness*, Eckhart expresses himself as follows upon the relation of the outer perception to the inner: "Here thou must know that the Masters say that in every man there are two kinds of man: the one is called the outer man, and yet he acts through the power of the soul. The other man is called the inner man, that is, that which is within the man. Now thou must know that every man who loveth God maketh no more use of the powers of the soul in the outer man than so far as the five senses absolutely require; and that which is within turns not itself to the five senses, save in so far as it is the guide and conductor of the five senses, and shepherds them, so that they follow not after their craving to bestiality." One who speaks in such wise of the inner man can no longer direct his gaze upon a Being of things lying outside himself; for he sees clearly that from no kind or species of the outer world can this Being come to him.

An objector might urge: What can it matter to the things of the outer world, what you add to them out of your own mind? Do but rely upon your own senses. They alone give you information of the outer world. Do not adulterate, by a mental addition, what your senses give you in purity, without admixture, as the image of the outer world. Your eye tells you what colour is; what your mind knows about colour, of that there is nothing whatever in colour itself. To this, from Meister Eckhart's standpoint, the answer would have to be: The senses are a physical apparatus; therefore what they have to tell us about objects can concern only that which is physical in the objects. And this physical factor in the objects communicates itself to me in such wise that in myself a physical process is set going.

Colour, as a physical process of the outer world, sets up a physical process in my eye and brain. Thereby I perceive colour. But in this manner I can perceive of colour only so much as is physical, sensuous. Sense-perception cuts out everything non-sensuous from objects. Objects are thus by sense-perception stripped of everything about them which is non-sensuous. If I then advance to the spiritual, the ideal content, I in fact only reinstate in the objects what sense-perception has shut out therefrom. Thus sense-perception does not exhibit to me the deepest Being of objects, it rather separates me from that being. But the spiritual, the ideal conception, seizing upon them again, unites me with that being. It shows me that objects are inwardly of exactly the same spiritual (*geistigen*) nature as I myself.

The barrier between myself and the outer world falls through this spiritual conception of things. I am separated from the external world in so far as I am a thing of the senses among other things of the senses. Colour and my eye are two different entities. My brain and a plant are two different things. But the ideal content of the plant and of colour belong together with the ideal content of my brain and eye alike to a single ideal entity.

This way of looking at things must not be confused with the very widespread anthropomorphising conception of the world, which imagines that it grasps the objects of the outer world by ascribing to them qualities of a physical nature, which are supposed to resemble the qualities of the human soul. This view asserts: When we meet another human being, we perceive in him only sensuous characteristics. I cannot see into my fellow-man's inner life. I infer from what I see and hear of him, his inner life, his soul. Thus the soul is never anything which I can directly perceive; I perceive a soul only within myself. My thoughts, my imaginations, my feelings, no man sees. Now just as I have such an inner life, alongside of the life which can be outwardly perceived, so, too, all other beings must have such an inner life.

Thus concludes one who occupies the standpoint of the anthropomorphising conception of the world. What I perceive externally in the plant, must equally be the outer side of something inward, of a soul, which I must add in my imagination to what I actually perceive. And since for me there exists but one single inner world, namely, my own, therefore I can conceive of the inner world of other beings only as resembling my own inner world. Along this line of argument one comes to a sort of universal ensouling of all nature (Pan-psychism).

This view depends, however, on a failure to recognise what the awakened inner sense really gives us. The spiritual (*geistig*) content of an external object, which reveals itself to me in my inner self, is not anything added in or by thought to the outer perception. It is just as little this as is the spirit of another man. I perceive this spiritual content through the inner sense just in the same way as I perceive its physical content through the external senses. And what I call my inner life in the above sense (*i.e.*, thoughts, feelings, etc.), is not at all in the higher sense, my spirit (*Geist*). This so-called inner life is only the outcome of purely sensuous processes, and belongs to me only as a purely individual personality, which is nothing more than the result of its physical organisation. If I transfer this inner life to outer things, I am, as a matter of fact, thinking in the air.

My personal soul-life, my thoughts, memories, and feelings, are in me, because I am a nature-being organised in such and such a way, with a perfectly definite sense-apparatus, with a perfectly definite nervous system. I have no right to transfer this my human soul to other things. I should only be entitled to do so if I happened to find anywhere a similarly organised nervous system. But my individual soul is not the highest spiritual element in me. This highest spiritual element must first be awakened through the inner sense; and this awakened spiritual element in me is also one and the same with the spiritual element in all things. The plant appears immediately in its own proper spirituality to this spiritual element,—I have no need to endow it with a spirituality like unto my own.

All talk about the unknown "thing-in-itself" loses any kind of meaning with this conception of the world; for it is just that very "thing-in-itself" which reveals itself to the inner sense. All such talk originates simply in the fact that those who talk thus are unable to recognise in the spiritual contents of their own inner being the "things-in-themselves." They think that they know in their own inner selves mere shadows and schemes without being,—"mere concepts and ideas" of things. But as they still have a sort of premonition of the "thing-in-itself," they therefore believe that this "thing-in-itself" is concealing itself, and that there are limits set to man's power of knowing. One cannot prove to such as are entangled in this belief, that they must grasp the "thing-in-itself" in their own inner being, for even if one were to put it before them, they would still never recognise or admit this "thing-in-itself." But it is just this recognition with which we are concerned.

All that Meister Eckhart says is saturated with this recognition. "Of this take a comparison: A door opens and shuts upon a hinge. If, now, I compare the outer plank of this door to the outer man, I must then compare the hinge to the inner man. Now, when the door opens and shuts, the outer plank moves to and fro, while yet the hinge remains constantly immovable and is in no way changed thereby. In like manner it is here also." As an individual sense-being, I can investigate things in all directions—the door opens and shuts,—if I do not spiritually give birth within me to the perceptions of the senses, then do I know nothing of their nature—the hinge does not move!

The illumination brought about through the inner sense is, according to Eckhart's view, the entrance of God into the soul. The light of knowledge which flames up through this entrance, he calls the "little spark of the soul." The point in man's inner being at which this "spark" flames up is "so pure, so lofty, and so noble in itself, that no creature can be therein, but only God alone dwells therein with His purely Divine Nature." Whosoever has kindled this "spark" in himself, no longer sees only as sees the ordinary man with his outer senses, and with his logical understanding which orders and classifies the impressions of the senses, but he sees how things are in themselves. The outer senses and the classifying understanding separate the individual man from other things; they make of him an individual in space and time, who also perceives the other things in space and time. The man illuminated by the "spark" ceases to be a single separated being. He annihilates his separateness. All that brings about the difference between himself and things ceases to be. That he, as a single being, is that which perceives, no longer comes into consideration. Things and he himself are no longer separated. Things, and with them, God, see themselves in him. "This spark is in very deed God, in that it is a single oneness and bears within it the imagery of all creatures, image without image, and image upon image."

Eckhart proclaims in the most magnificent words the extinction of the isolated being: "It is therefore to be known, that according to things it is one and the same to know God and to be known by God. Therein do we know God and see, that He makes us to see and to know. And as the air, which enlighteneth, is nothing other than what it enlightens; for the air giveth light, because it is enlightened; even so do we know that we are known, and that He maketh us to know Himself."

On this foundation Meister Eckhart builds up his relation to God. It is a purely spiritual one, and cannot be modelled according to any image borrowed from human individual experience. Not as one separated individual loves another can God love his creation: not as an architect builds a house can God have created it. All such thoughts vanish before the inner vision. It belongs to God's very being that He should love the world. A God who could love or not love at pleasure, is imagined according to the likeness of the individual man. "I speak in good truth and in eternal truth and in everlasting truth, that God must needs ever pour Himself forth in every man who has reached down to his true root to the utmost of possibility, so wholly and completely that in His life and in His being, in His nature and in His Godhead, He keeps nothing back; He must ever pour all forth in fruitful wise." And the inner illumination is something that the soul must necessarily find when it sinks itself deep into the basis of its being.

From this it is already obvious that God's communication to humanity cannot be conceived after the fashion of the revelation of one human being to another. This communication may also be cut off, for one man can shut himself off from another; but God *must*, by virtue of His very nature, reveal Himself. "It is a sure and certain truth, that it is a necessity for God to seek us, exactly as if His very Godhead depended upon it. God can as little dispense with us as we with Him. Even though we turn away from God, yet God can never turn away from us." Consequently, man's relation to God cannot be conceived of as though something image-like, something taken from the individual human being, were contained therein.

Eckhart is thus conscious that it belongs to the perfectness of the Root-Being of the world to find Itself in the human soul. This Root-Being indeed would be imperfect, incomplete, if it lacked that part of its unfoldment which comes to light in the soul. What happens in man belongs to the Root-Being; and if it did not happen, then the Root-

Being would be but a part of Itself. In this sense, man can feel himself as a necessary part of the Being of the universe. This Eckhart expresses by describing his feelings towards God as follows: "I thank not God that He loveth me, for He may not do otherwise; whether He will it or no, His nature yet compelleth Him.... Therefore will I not pray to God to give me anything, nor will I praise Him for that which He hath given me..."

But this relationship of the soul to the Root-Being must not be conceived of as if the soul in its individual nature were declared to be identical with this Root-Being. The soul which is entangled in the sense-world, and so in the finite, has as such not yet got within itself the content of the Root-Being. The soul must first develop that content within itself. It must annihilate itself as an isolated being; and Meister Eckhart most aptly characterises this annihilation as *Entwerdung* (un-becoming or involution). "When I come to the root of the Godhead, none ask me whence I come and where I have been, and none doth miss me, for here there is an *Entwerdung*." Again, the following phrase speaks very clearly about this relation: "I take a cup of water and lay therein a mirror and set it under the disc of the sun. The sun casts out its shining light on the mirror and yet doth not pass away. The reflecting of the mirror in the sun is sun in the sun, and yet the mirror remains what it is. So is it about God. God is in the soul with His very nature and being and Godhead, and yet He is not the soul. The reflecting of the soul in God, is God in God, and yet the soul is still that which it is."

The soul which gives itself up to the inner illumination knows in itself not only what this same soul was before its illumination; but it also knows that which this soul only became through this illumination. "We must be united with God in being; we must be united with God uniquely; we must be united with God wholly. How shall we be united with God in being? That must happen in the beholding and not in the *Wesung*. His being may not become our being, but it shall be our life." Not an already existent life—a *Wesung*—is to be known in the logical sense; but the higher knowing—the beholding—shall itself become life; the spiritual, the ideal must be so felt by the beholder, as ordinary daily life is felt by individual human nature.

From such starting points, Meister Eckhart also builds up a pure conception of Freedom. In its ordinary life the soul is not free; for it is interwoven with the realm of lower causes, and accomplishes that to which it is impelled by these lower causes. But by "beholding" or "vision" it is raised out of the domain of these causes, and acts no longer as a separated individual soul. The root of being is laid bare in this soul, and that can be moved to action by naught save by itself. "God does not compel the will; rather He sets the will free, so that it wills not otherwise than what God Himself wills; and the spirit desires not to will other than what God wills: and that is not its un-freedom: it is its true and real freedom. For freedom is that we are not bound, but free and pure and unmixed, as we were in our first outpouring, as we were set free in the Holy Ghost."

It may be said of the illuminated man that he is himself the being which from within itself determines what is good and what is evil. He can do naught absolutely, but accomplish the good. For he does not serve the good, but the good realises and lives itself out in him. "The righteous man serveth neither God, nor the creature; for he is free, and the nearer he is to righteousness, the more he is Freedom's very self." What then, for Meister Eckhart, can evil be? It can be only action under the influence of the lower mode of regarding things;—the acting of a soul which has not passed through the state of *Entwerdung* (un-becoming). Such a soul is selfish in the sense that it wills only itself. It could not bring its willing outwardly into accord with moral ideals. The soul having vision cannot in this sense be selfish. Even if it willed itself, it yet could will only the lordship of the ideal; for it has made itself into this very ideal. It can no longer will the ends of the lower nature, for it has no longer aught in common with this lower nature. To act in conformity with moral ideals implies for the soul which has vision, no compulsion, no deprivation.

"The man who standeth in God's will and in God's love, to him it is a craving to do all good things that God willeth, and leave undone all evil things that are contrary to God. And it is impossible for him to leave undone anything that God will have done. Even as walking is impossible to one whose legs are bound, just so it would be impossible for a man who standeth in God's will to do aught unvirtuous."

Eckhart moreover expressly guards himself against the idea that, with this view of his, free license is given for anything and everything that the individual may will. The man possessing vision is indeed to be recognised by the very fact that as a separated individual he no longer wills anything. "Certain men say: If I have God and God's freedom, then I may just do whatever I please. Such understand wrongly this saying. So long as thou canst do aught that is contrary to God and His commandment, so long thou hast not God's love; even though thou mayest well deceive the world, as if thou hadst." Eckhart is convinced that to the soul which dives down into its own root, the most perfect morality will shine forth from that root to meet it; that there all logical conception, and all acting in the ordinary sense, ceases, and an entirely new ordering of human life makes its appearance.

"For all that the understanding can grasp, and all that desiring can desire, is verily not God. Where understanding and desiring end, there it is dark, there shineth God. There that power unfolds in the soul which is wider than the wide heavens. . . . The bliss of the righteous and the bliss of God is one bliss; for there is the righteous full of bliss, where God is full of bliss."

THE FRIENDSHIP OF GOD (TAULER, SUSO AND RUYSBROECK)

In Johannes Tauler (1300-1361), Heinrich Suso (1295-1365), and Johannes Ruysbroeck (1293-1381), one makes acquaintance with men whose life and work exhibit in a very striking manner those "motions of the soul" to which such a spiritual path as that of Meister Eckhart is calculated to give rise in natures of depth and power. While Eckhart seems like a man who, in the blissful experiencing of spiritual re-birth, speaks of the nature of Knowledge as of a picture which he has succeeded in painting; these others, followers of his, appear rather like pilgrims, to whom their inner re-birth has shown a new road which they fain would tread, but whose goal seems to vanish before them into the illimitable distance. Eckhart dwells more upon the glories of his picture; they upon the difficulties of the new path.

To understand the difference between personalities like Eckhart and Tauler, one must see quite clearly how a man stands towards his higher cognitions. Man is interwoven with the sense-world and the laws of nature by which that sense-world is ruled. He is himself a product of that world. He lives because its forces and its materials are at work in him; nay, he perceives this sense-world and judges of it by laws, according to which both he himself and that world are alike built up. If he turns his eyes upon an object, not only does the object present itself to him as a complex of interacting forces, ruled by nature's laws, but the eye, with which he sees the object is itself a body built up according to just such laws and of just such forces; and the seeing, too, takes place by similar laws and forces. If we had reached the goal of natural science, we should be able to follow out this play of the forces of nature according to natural laws right up into the highest regions of thought-formation, —but in the very act of doing this, we raise ourselves *above* this play of forces. For do we not stand above and beyond all the "uniformities which make up the laws of nature," when we over-see the whole and recognise how we ourselves fit into nature? We *see* with our eyes according to laws of nature. But we know also the laws, according to which we see.

We can take our stand upon a higher summit and overlook at once both ourselves and the outer world in their mutual interplay. Is there not here a something working in us, which is higher than the sensuous-organic personality working with Nature's forces and according to Nature's laws? In such activity does there still remain any wall of division between our inner selves and the outer world? That which here judges and gains for itself insight is no longer our separated personality; it is rather the general world-being, which has torn down the barrier between the inner and outer worlds and now embraces both alike. As true as it is that, judged by the outer appearance, I still remain the same separated individual when I have thus torn down this barrier, so true is it also that, judged according to essential being, I am no longer this separated unit. Henceforth there lives in me the feeling that there speaks in my soul the All-Being, which embraces both myself and the entire world.

This is what Tauler felt, when he said: "Man is just as if he were three men—his animal man as he is according to the senses; then his rational man and lastly, his highest, godlike man. . . . The one is the outer, animal, sensuous man; the other is the inner, understanding man, with his understanding and reasoning powers; the third man is spirit, (*Gemüth*—lit. emotional, feeling nature), the very highest part of the soul."* How far this third man is above the first and second, Eckhart has expressed in the words: "The eye through which I see God, that is the same eye with which God sees me. My eye and God's eye, that is one eye and one knowing and one feeling."

But in Tauler another feeling is active as well as this. He has fought

---

* *Cp.* W. Preger: *Geschichte der Deutschen Mystik, vol. iii, p. 161.*

his way through to a real vision of the spiritual, and does not constantly confuse, as do the false materialists and the false idealists, the sensibly-natural with the spiritual. If, with his disposition, Tauler had become a scientist, he would have insisted upon explaining all that is natural, including the *whole* of man, both the first and the second, purely upon natural lines. He would never have transferred purely spiritual forces into nature itself. He would never have talked of a "purposefulness" in nature conceived of according to men's notions. He knew that there, where we perceive with our senses, no "creative ideas" are to be found. Far rather he was most keenly conscious of the fact that man is a purely natural being. And as he felt himself to be, not a scientist, but a devotee of moral life, he therefore felt most keenly the contrast which reveals itself between this natural being of man and that vision of God which arises naturally and within nature, but as spirituality. And just in that very contrast the meaning of life presented itself to his eyes. Man finds himself as a single being, a creature of nature. And no science can reveal to him anything else about this life than that he is such a creature of nature. As a creature of nature he cannot get outside of the sphere of natural creation. In it he must remain. And yet his inner life leads him outside and beyond it. He must have confidence in that which no science of outer nature can give him or show to him.

If he calls only this nature Being or "that which is," then he must be able to reach out to the vision which recognises as the higher, Non-being, or "that which is not." Tauler seeks for no God who is present in the same sense as a natural force; he seeks no God who has created the world in the sense of human creation. In him lives the clear insight that the conception of creation even of the Fathers of the Church is only idealised human creating. It is clear to him that God is not to be found as nature's working and her laws are found, by science. Tauler is well aware that we must not add in thought anything to nature as God. He knows that whoever thinks God, in his sense, no longer thinks thought-content, as does one who has grasped nature in thought. Therefore, Tauler seeks not to think God, but to think divinely, to think as God thinks. The knowledge of nature is not *enriched* by the knowledge of God, but *transformed*. The knower of God does not know a different thing from the knower of nature, but he knows in a different way. Not one single letter can the knower of God add to the knowledge of nature; but through his whole knowing of nature there shines a new light.

What root-feelings will take possession of a man's soul who contemplates the world from this point of view, will depend upon how he regards that experience of the soul which brings about spiritual re-birth. Within this experience, man is wholly a natural being, when he considers himself in his interaction with the rest of nature; and he is wholly a spiritual being when he considers the conditions into which this re-birth has brought him. Thus we can say with equal truth, the inmost depth of the soul is still natural; as also it is already divine. Tauler emphasised the former in accordance with his own tendency of thought. However far we may penetrate into our souls, we still remain separated individual human beings, said he to himself. But yet in the very depths of the soul of the individual being there gleams forth the All-Being.

Tauler was dominated by the feeling: Thou canst not free thyself from separateness, nor purify thyself from it. Therefore the All-Being in its purity can never make its appearance within thee, it can only shed its light into the depths of thy soul. Thus in its depths only a mere reflection, a picture of the All-Being comes into existence. Thou canst so transform thy separated personality that it reproduces the All-Being as a picture; but this All-Being itself does not shine forth in thee. Starting from such conceptions, Tauler came to the idea of a Godhead that never merges wholly into the human world, never flows quite completely into it. More, he attaches importance to his not being confused with those who maintain that man's inmost being is itself divine. He says: "The Union with God is taken by foolish men in a fleshly sense, and they say that they shall be transformed into divine nature; but such is false and an evil heresy. For even in the very highest, most inward Union with God, God's nature and God's being still remain lofty, yea, higher than the loftiest; that passeth into a divine abyss, where never yet was creature."

Tauler wishes, and rightly, to be called a good Catholic in the sense of his age and of his priestly calling. He has no desire to oppose any other conception to Christianity. He desires only to deepen and spiritualise that Christianity through his way of looking at it. He speaks as a pious priest of the content of Holy Writ. But this same scripture still becomes in the world of his conceptions a means for the expression of the inmost experiences of his soul. "God worketh all his works in the soul and giveth them to the soul; and the Father begetteth His only begotten Son in the soul, as truly as He begetteth Him in eternity, neither more, nor less. What is born when one says: God begetteth in the soul? Is it a likeness of God, or a picture of God, or is it somewhat of God? Nay: it is neither picture nor likeness of God, but the same God and the same Son whom the Father begetteth in eternity and naught else than the blissful divine word, that is the second person in the Trinity, Him the Father begetteth in the soul, ... and thereof the soul hath thus great and special dignity."* The stories of scripture become for Tauler the garment in which he clothes the happiness of the inner life. "Herod, who drove out the child and sought to slay him, is a likeness of the world, which yet seeketh to kill this child in a believing man, therefore one should and must flee therefrom, if we do desire to keep that child alive in us, but that child is the enlightened believing soul of each and every man."

As Tauler directs his gaze mainly upon the natural man, he is comparatively less concerned to tell us what happens when the higher man enters into the natural man, than to discover the paths which the lower forces of the personality must follow if they are to be transmuted into the higher life. As a devotee of the moral life, he desires to show to men the roads to the All-Being. He has unconditional faith and trust that the All-Being shines forth in man, if man will so order his life that there shall be in him a shrine for the Divine. But this All-Being can never shine forth while man shuts himself up in his mere natural separated personality. Such a man, separated off in himself, is merely one member of the world: a single creature, in Tauler's language. The more man shuts himself off within this his being as a member of the world, so much the less can the All-Being find place in him. "If man is in reality to become one with God, then all energies and powers even of the inner man must die and become silent. The will must turn away even from the Good and from all willing, and become void of willing." "Man must escape from all his senses and turn inwards all his powers, and come into a forgetting of all things and of himself." "For the true and eternal Word of God is uttered only in the desert, when the man hath gone out from himself and from all things and is quite untrammelled, desolate and alone."

When Tauler stood at his zenith, the problem which occupied the central point of his mental life was: How can man overcome and kill out

---

* Cp. Preger: *History of German Mysticism, vol. iii., p. 219 et seq.*

in himself his separated existence, so as to live in perfect unison with the All-life? For one in this position, all feelings towards the All-Being concentrate themselves into this one thing: Awe before the All-Being as that which is inexhaustible, endless. He says to himself: whatever level thou hast reached, there remain still higher perspectives, still more exalted possibilities. Thus clear and defined as is to him the direction in which he has to turn his steps, it is equally clear to him that he can never speak of a goal: for a new goal is only the beginning of a new path. Through such a new goal man reaches a certain level of evolution: but evolution itself continues illimitably. And what that evolution may attain upon some more distant level, it can never know upon its present stage. There is no *knowing* the final goal: only a *trusting* in the path, in evolution itself. There is knowing for everything which man has already attained. It consists in the penetration of an already present object by the powers of our spirit. For the higher life of man's inner being, there is no such knowing. Here the powers of our spirit must first transfer the object itself into the realm of the existent; they must first create for it an existence, constituted as is natural existence.

Natural Science follows the evolution of beings from the simplest up to the most perfected, to man himself. This evolution lies before us as already completed. We know it, by penetrating it with the powers of our spirit. When evolution has reached humanity, man then finds nothing further there before him as its continuation. He himself accomplishes the further unfoldment. Henceforward he *lives* what for earlier stages he only *knows*. He creates, according to the object, that which, for what has gone before, he only copies in accordance with its spiritual nature. That truth is not one with the existent in nature, but naturally embraces both the existent and the non-existent: of this truth Tauler is filled to overflowing in all his feelings. It has been handed down to us that Tauler was led to this fulfilling by an illuminated layman, a "Friend of God from the Mountains."

We have here a mysterious story. As to where this "Friend of God" lived there exist only conjectures; as to who he was, not even these. He seems to have heard much of Tauler's way of preaching, and to have resolved accordingly to journey to Tauler, who was then working as a preacher in Strasbourg, in order to fulfil a certain duty by him. Tauler's relation to the Friend of God, and the influence which the latter exercised upon the former, are to be found described in a text which is printed along with the oldest editions of Tauler's sermons under the title, "The Book of the Master." Therein a Friend of God, in whom some seek to recognise the same who came into relations with Tauler, gives an account of a "Master," whom some assert to be Tauler himself. He relates how a transformation, a spiritual re-birth, was brought about in a certain "Master" and how the latter, when he felt his death drawing near, called his friend to him and begged him to write the story of his "enlightenment," but yet to take care that no one should ever learn of whom the book speaks. He asks this on the ground that all the knowledge that proceeds from him is yet not really from him. "For know ye that God hath brought all to pass through me, poor worm, and that what it is, is not mine, it is of God."

A learned controversy which has connected itself with the occurrence is not of the very smallest importance for the essence of the matter. An effort was made to prove on one side[*] that the Friend of God never existed, but that his existence was fiction and that the books ascribed to him come from another hand (Rulman Merswin). On the other hand Wilhelm Preger has sought with many arguments (in his *History of German Mysticism*) to support the existence, the genuineness of the writings, and the correctness of the facts that relate to Tauler.

I am here under no obligation to throw light by presumptuous investigation upon a relationship as to which any one, who understands how to read the writings[†] in question, will know that it should remain a secret.

If one says of Tauler, that at a certain stage of his life a transformation took place in him, that will be amply sufficient. Tauler's personality need no longer be in any way considered in this connection, but only a personality "in general." As regards Tauler, we are only concerned with the fact that we must understand his transformation from the point of view set forth in what follows. If we compare his later activity with his earlier, the fact of this transformation is obvious without further search. I will leave aside all outer circumstances and relate the inner occurrences

---

[*] Denifle: *Die Dichtungen des Gottesfreundes im Oberlande.*
[†] The writings in question are, among others: *Von eime eigenwilligen weltwisen manne, der von eime heiligen weltpriestere gewiset wart uffe demuetige gehorsamme, 1338; Das Buch von den zwei Mannen; Der gefangene Ritter, 1349; Die geistliche stege , 1350; Von der geistlichen Leiter, 1357; Das Meisterbuch, 1369; Geschichte von zwei fünfzehnjährigen Knaben.*

in the soul of the "Master" under "the influence of the layman." What my reader will understand by the "layman" and the "Master" depends entirely upon his own mentality; what I myself think about it is a matter as to which I cannot know for whom it is of any weight.

A Master is instructing his disciples as to the relationship of the soul to the All-Being of things. He speaks of the fact that when man plunges into the abysmal depths of his soul, he no longer feels the natural, limited forces of the separated personality working within him. Therein the separated man no longer speaks, therein speaks God. There man does not see God, or the world; there God sees Himself. Man has become one with God. But the Master knows that this teaching has not yet awakened to full life in him. He thinks it with his understanding: but he does not yet live in it with every fibre of his personality. He is thus teaching about a state of things which he has not yet completely lived through in himself. The description of the condition corresponds to the truth; yet this truth has no value if it does not gain life, if it does not bring itself forth in reality as actually existent.

The "layman" or "Friend of God" hears of the Master and his teachings. He is no less saturated with the truth which the Master utters than the Master himself. But he possesses this truth not as a matter of the understanding; he has it as the whole force of his life. He knows that when this truth has come to a man from outside, he can himself give utterance to it, without even in the least living in accordance with it. But in that case he has nothing other in him than the natural knowledge of the understanding. He then speaks of this natural knowledge as if it were the highest, equivalent to the working of the All-Being. It is not so, because it has not been acquired in a life that has approached to this knowledge as a transformed, a reborn life. What one acquires only as a natural man, that remains only natural,—even when one afterwards expresses in words the fundamental characteristic of the higher knowledge. Outwards, from within the very nature itself, must the transformation be accomplished.

Nature, which by living has evolved itself to a certain level, must evolve further through life; something new must come into existence through this further evolution. Man must not only look backwards upon the evolution which already lies behind him—claim as the highest that which shapes itself according thereto in his spirit—but he must look forward upon the uncreate: his knowledge must be a beginning of a new content, not an end to the content of evolution which already lies before it. Nature advances from the worm to the mammal, from the mammal to man, not in a conceptual but in an actual, real process. Man has to repeat this process not in his mind alone. The mental repetition is only the beginning of a fresh, real evolution, which, however, despite its being spiritual, is real. Man, then, does not merely know what nature has produced; he continues nature; he translates his knowledge into living action. He gives birth within himself to the spirit, and this spirit advances thence onwards from level to level of evolution, as nature itself advances. Spirit begins a natural process upon a higher level.

The talk about the God who contemplates Himself in man's inner being, takes on a different character in one who has recognised this. He attaches little importance to the fact that an insight already attained has led him into the depths of the All-Being; instead, his spiritual nature acquires a new character. It unfolds itself further in the direction determined by the All-Being. Such a man not only looks at the world differently from one who merely understands: he lives his life otherwise. He does not talk of the meaning which life already has through the forces and laws of the world: but he gives anew a fresh meaning to his life. As little as the fish already has in itself what makes its appearance on a later level of evolution as the mammal, as little has the understanding man already in himself what shall be born from him as the higher man. If the fish could know itself and the things around it, it would regard the being-a-fish as the meaning of life. It would say: the All-Being is like the fish: in the fish the All-Being beholds itself. Thus would the fish speak as long as it remained constant to its understanding kind of knowledge. In reality it does not remain constant thereto. It reaches out beyond its knowledge with its activity. It becomes a reptile and later a mammal. The meaning which it gives to itself in reality reaches out beyond the meaning which mere contemplation gives to it.

In man also this must be so. He gives himself a meaning in reality; he does not halt and stand still at the meaning he already has, which his contemplation shows him. Knowledge leaps out beyond itself, if only it understands itself aright. Knowledge cannot deduce the world from a ready-made God; it can only unfold itself from a germ in the direction towards a God. The man who has understood this will not regard God as something that is outside of him; he will deal with God as a being who wanders with him towards a goal, which at the outset is just as unknown as the nature of the mammal is unknown to the fish. He does not aim to be the knower of the hidden, or of the self-revealing existent God, but to be the friend of the divine doing and working, which is exalted over both being and non-being.

The layman, who came to the Master, was a "Friend of God" in this sense, and through him the Master became from a contemplator of the being of God, one who is "alive in the spirit," one who not only contemplated, but lived in the higher sense. The Master now no longer brought forth concepts and ideas of the understanding from his inner nature, but these concepts and ideas burst forth from him as living, actualised spirit. He no longer merely edified his hearers; he shook the very foundations of their being. He no longer plunged their souls into their inner being; he led them into a new life. This is recounted to us symbolically: about forty people fell down through his preaching and lay as if dead.

～

As a guide to such a new life, we possess a book about whose author nothing is known. Luther first made it known in print. The philologist, Franz Pfeiffer, has recently printed it according to a manuscript of the year 1497, with a modern German translation facing the original text. What precedes the book indicates its purpose and its goal: "Here begins the man from Frankfurt and saith many very lofty and very beautiful things about a perfect life." Upon this follows the "Preface about the man from Frankfurt": "Al-mighty, Eternal God hath uttered this little book through a wise, understanding, truthful, righteous man, his friend, who in former days was a German nobleman, a priest and a custodian in the German House of Nobles at Frankfurt; it teacheth many a lovely insight into Divine Wisdom, and especially how and whereby one may know the true, righteous friends of God, and also the unrighteous, false, free-thinkers, who are very hurtful to Holy Church."

By "free-thinkers" one may perhaps understand those who live in a merely conceptual world, like the "Master" described above before his transformation by means of the "Friend of God," and by the "true, righteous friends of God," such as possess the disposition of the "layman." One may further ascribe to the book the intention of so working upon its readers as the "Friend of God from the Mountains" did upon the Master. It is not known who the author was. But what does that mean? It is not known when he was born and died, or what he did in his outer life. That the author aimed to preserve eternal secrecy about these facts of his outer life, belongs naturally to the way in which he desired to work. It is not the "I" of this or the other man, born at a definite point of time, who is to speak to us, but the "I-ness" in the depths whereof "the separateness of individualities" (in the sense of Paul Asmus' saying*) must first unfold itself. "If God took to Himself all men who are or who have ever been, and became man in them, and they became God in Him, and it did not happen to me also, then my fall and my turning away would never be made good, unless it also happened in me too. And in this restoration and making good, I neither can nor may nor should do anything thereto save a mere pure suffering, so that God alone doeth and worketh all things in me, and I suffer Him and all His works and His divine will. But if I will not submit to this, but possess myself with egotism, *i.e.*, with mine, and I, to me, for me, and the like, that hinders God so that He cannot work His work in me purely alone and without hindrance. Therefore my fall and my turning away remain thus not made good." The "man from Frankfurt" aims to speak not as a separated individual; he desires to let God speak. That he yet can do this only as a single, distinct personality he naturally knows full well; but he is a "Friend of God," that means a man who aims not at presenting the nature of life through contemplation, but at pointing out the beginning of a new evolutionary pathway through the living spirit.

The explanations in the book are various instructions as to how one comes to this pathway. The root-thought returns again and again: man must strip off everything that is connected with that which makes him appear as a single, separate personality. This thought seems to be worked out only in respect of the moral life; it should be extended, without further ado, to the higher life of knowledge as well. One must annihilate in oneself whatever appears as separateness: then separated existence ceases; the All-Life enters into us. We cannot master this All-Life by drawing it towards us. It comes into us, when we reduce the separateness in us to silence. We have the All-Life least of all just then, when we so regard our separated existence as if the Whole already dwelt within it. This first comes to light in the separated existence when this separated

---

* *Vide ante.*

existence no longer claims for itself to be anything. This pretension on the part of the separated existence our text terms "assumption."

Through "assumption" the self makes it impossible for itself that the Universal Self should enter into it. The self then puts itself as a part, as something imperfect, in the place of the whole, of the perfect. "The perfect is a being, that in itself and in its being has conceived and resolved all beings, and without which and apart from which there is no true being, and in which all things have their being; for it is the being of all things and is in itself unchangeable and immovable, and changes and moves all other things. But the divided and the imperfect is that which has sprung from out of this perfect, or becomes, just as a ray or a light that flows forth from the sun or a light and shines upon something, this or that. And that is called the creature, and of all these divided things none is the perfect. Therefore also is the perfect none of the divided.... When the perfect cometh, the divided is despised. But when does it come? I say: When so far as is possible it is known, felt, tasted in the soul; for the defect lies wholly in us and not in it. For just as the sun illuminates the whole world and is just as near to the one as to the other, yet a blind man sees it not. But that is no defect of the sun but of the blind man.... If my eye is to see anything, it must become cleansed, or be already cleansed from all other things.... Now one might be inclined to say: In so far then as it is unknowable and inconceivable for all creatures, and since the soul is also a creature, how can it then be known in the soul? Answer: Therefore is it said, the creature shall be known *as a creature*."

This is as much as to say that all creatures shall be regarded as created and creation and not regard themselves as I-ness and self-ness, whereby this knowing is made impossible. "For in whatever creature this perfect one shall be known, there all creature-being, created-being, I-ness, self-ness, and everything of the kind must be lost, be and become naught."* The soul must therefore look within itself; there it finds its I-ness, its self-ness. If it remains standing there, it thereby cuts itself off from the perfect. If it regards its I-ness only as a thing lent to it as it were, and annihilates it in spirit, it will be seized upon by the stream of the All-Life, of Perfection. "When the creature assumes to itself somewhat of good, as Being, Life, Knowledge, Power, in short, aught of that

---

* Chap. i., *Book of the Man from Frankfurt*.

which one calls good and thinks that it is that, or that it belongs to it or comes from it, so often and so much as that happens, does the creature turn away." "The created soul of man has two eyes. The one is the possibility of seeing in eternity; the other of seeing in time and in creation." "Man should therefore stand and be quite free without himself, that is without self-ness, I-ness, me, mine, for me and the like, so that he as little seeks and thinks of himself and what is his in all things as if it did not exist; and he should therefore also think little of himself, as if he were not, and as if another had done all his deeds."*

One must also take account of the fact in regard to the writer of these sentences, that the thought-content, to which he gives a direction by his higher ideas and feelings, is that of a believing priest in the spirit of his own time. We are here concerned not with the thought-content, but with the direction, not with the thoughts but with the way of thinking. Any one who does not live as he does in Christian dogmas, but in the conceptions of natural science, finds in his sentences other thoughts; but with these other thoughts he points in the same direction. And this direction is that which leads to the overcoming of the self-hood, by the Self-hood itself. The highest light shines for man in his Ego. But this light only then imparts to his concept-world the right reflection, when he becomes aware that it is not his own self-light, but the universal world-light.

Hence there is no more important knowledge than self-knowledge; and there is equally no knowledge which leads so completely out beyond itself. When the "self" knows itself aright, it is already no longer a "self." In his own language, the writer of the book in question expresses this as follows: "For God's 'own-ness' is void of this and that, void of self-ness and I-ness; but the nature and own-ness of the creature is that it seeketh and willeth itself and its own and 'this' and 'that'; and in all that it does or leaves undone, it seeketh to receive its own benefit and profit."

"When, now, the creature or the man loseth his own-ness and his self-ness and himself, and goeth out from himself, then God entereth in with His Own-ness, that is with his Self-hood."† Man soars upwards, from a view of his "Ego" which makes the latter appear to him as his

---

* Chap. xv., *Book of the Man from Frankfurt*.
† Chap. xxiv, *Book of the Man from Frankfurt*.

very being, to a view such that it shows him his Ego as a mere organ, in which the All-Being works upon itself. In the concept-sphere of our text, this means: "If man can attain thereto that he belongeth unto God just as a man's hand belongeth to him, then let him content himself and seek no further."* That is not intended to mean that when man has reached a certain stage of his evolution he shall stand still there, but that, when he has got as far as is indicated in the above words, he should not set on foot further investigations into the meaning of the hand, but rather make use of the hand, in order that it may render service to the body to which it belongs.

~

HEINRICH SUSO and JOHANNES RUYSBROEK possessed a type of mind which may be characterised as genius for feeling. Their feelings are drawn by something like instinct in the same direction in which Eckhart's and Tauler's feelings were guided by their higher thought-life. Suso's heart turns devoutly towards that Root-Being which embraces the individual man just as much as the whole remaining world, and in whom forgetting himself, he yearns to lose himself as a drop of water in the mighty ocean. He speaks of this his yearning towards the All-Being, not as of something that he desires to embrace in thought; he speaks of it as a natural impulse, that makes his soul drunken with desire for the annihilation of its separated existence and its re-awakening to life in the all-efficiency of the endless life. "Turn thine eyes to this being in its pure naked simplicity, so that thou mayest let fall this and that manifold being. Take being in itself alone, that is unmoved with not-being; for all not-being denies all being. A thing that is yet to become, or that has been, is not now in actual presence."

"Now, one cannot know mixed being or not-being except by some mark of being as a whole. For if one will understand a thing, the reason first encounters being, and that is a being that worketh all things. It is a divided being of this or that creature,—for divided being is all mingled with something of other-ness, with a possibility of receiving something. Therefore the nameless divine being must so be a *whole* being in itself, that it sustaineth all divided beings by its presence."

---

* *Ibid.*, Chap. liv.

Thus speaks Suso in the autobiography which he wrote in conjunction with his pupil Elsbet Stäglin. He, too, is a pious priest and lives entirely in the Christian circle of thought. He lives therein as if it were quite unthinkable that anybody with his mental tendency could live in any other world. But of him also it is true that one can combine another concept-content with his mental tendency. This is clearly borne out by the way in which the content of the Christian teaching has become for him actual inner experience, and his relation to Christ has become a relation between his own spirit and the eternal truth in a purely ideal, spiritual way.

He composed a *"Little Book of Eternal Wisdom."* In this he makes the "Eternal Wisdom" speak to its servant, in other words to himself: "Knowest thou me not? How art thou so cast down, or hast thou lost consciousness from agony of heart, my tender child? Behold it is I, merciful Wisdom, who have opened wide the abyss of fathomless compassion which yet is hidden from all the saints, tenderly to receive thee and all repentant hearts; it is I, sweet Eternal Wisdom, who was there poor and miserable, so as to bring thee to thy worthiness; it is I, who suffered bitter death, that I might make thee to live again! I stand here pale and bleeding and lovely, as I stood on the lofty gallows of the cross between the stern judgment of my Father and thee. It is I, thy brother; look, it is I, thy spouse! I have therefore wholly forgotten all thou hast done against me, as if it had never been, if only thou turnest wholly to me and separatest thyself no more from me."

All that is bodily and temporal in the Christian conception has become for Suso, as one sees, a spiritual-ideal process in the recesses of his soul. From some chapters of Suso's biography mentioned above, it might appear as if he had let himself be guided not by the mere action of his own spiritual power, but through external revelations, through ghostly visions. But he expresses his meaning quite clearly about this. One attains to the truth through reasonableness, not through any kind of revelation. "The difference between pure truth and two-souled visions in the matter of knowledge I will also tell you. An immediate beholding of the bare Godhead, that is right pure truth, without all doubt; and every vision, so that it be reasonable and without pictures and the more like it be unto that bare beholding, the purer and nobler it is."

Meister Eckhart, too, leaves no doubt that he puts aside the view which seeks to be spiritual in bodily-spacial forms, in appearances which one can perceive by any senses. Minds of the type of Suso and Eckhart are thus opponents of such a view, as that which finds expression in the spiritualism which has developed during the nineteenth century.

~

JOHANNES RUYSBROEK, the Belgian mystic, trod the same path as Suso. His spiritual way found an active opponent in Johannes Gerson (born 1363), who was for some time Chancellor of the University of Paris and played a momentous rôle at the Council of Constance. Some light is thrown upon the nature of the mysticism which was practised by Tauler, Suso and Ruysbroek, if one compares it with the mystic endeavours of Gerson, who had his predecessors in Richard de St. Victor, Bonaventura, and others.

Ruysbroek himself fought against those whom he reckoned among the heretical mystics. As such he considered all those who, through an easy-going judgment of the understanding, hold that all things proceed from one Root-Being, who therefore see in the world only a manifoldness and in God the unity of this manifoldness. Ruysbroek does not count himself among these, for he knew that one cannot attain to the Root-Being by the contemplation of things, but only by raising oneself from this lower mode of contemplation to a higher one.

Similarly, he turned against those who seek to see without further ado, in the individual man, in his separated existence (in his creature-being), his higher nature also. He deplored not a little the error which confuses all differences in the sense-world, and asserts light-mindedly that things are different only in appearance, but that in their being they are all alike. This would amount, for a way of thinking like Ruysbroek's, to the same thing as saying: That the fact that the trees in an avenue seem to our seeing to come together does not concern us. In reality they are everywhere equally far apart, therefore our eyes ought to accustom themselves to see correctly. But our eyes see aright. That the trees run together depends upon a necessary law of nature; and we have nothing to reproach our seeing with, but on the contrary to recognise in spirit why we see them thus.

Moreover, the mystic does not turn away from the things of the senses. As things of the senses, he accepts them as they are, and it is clear to him that through no judgment of the understanding can they become otherwise. But in spirit he passes beyond both senses and understanding, and then only does he find the unity. His faith is unshakable that he can develop himself to the beholding of this unity. Therefore does he ascribe to the nature of man the divine spark which can be brought to shine in him, to shine by its own light.

People of the type of Gerson think otherwise. They do not believe in this self-shining. For them, what man can behold remains always a something external, that from some side or other must come to them externally. Ruysbroek believed that the highest wisdom must needs shine forth for mystic contemplation. Gerson believed only that the soul can illuminate the content of an external teaching (that of the Church). For Gerson, Mysticism was nothing else but possessing a warm feeling for everything that is revealed in this teaching. For Ruysbroek, it was a faith, that the content of all teaching is also born in the soul. Therefore Gerson blames Ruysbroek in that the latter imagines that not only has he the power to behold the All-Being with clearness, but that in this beholding there expresses itself an activity of the All-Being. Ruysbroek simply could not be understood by Gerson. Both spoke of two wholly different things. Ruysbroek has in his mind's eye the life of the soul that lives itself into oneness with its God; Gerson, only a soul-life that seeks to love the God whom it can never actually live in itself. Like many others, Gerson fought against something that was strange to him only because he could not grasp it in experience.

CARDINAL NICHOLAS OF CUSA

A gloriously shining star in the sky of the thought-life of the Middle Ages is Nicholas Chrysippus of Cusa (at Trevis, 1401-1464). He stands upon the summit of the knowledge of his time. In mathematics he accomplished remarkable work. In natural science he may be described as the forerunner of Copernicus, for he took up the standpoint that the earth is a moving celestial body like others. He had already broken away from a view upon which even a hundred years later the great astronomer, Tycho Brahe, based himself, when he hurled against the teaching of Copernicus the sentence: "The earth is a gross, heavy mass inapt for movement; how, then, can Copernicus make a star of it and run it about in the air?" The same man who thus not only embraced all the knowledge of his time, but also extended it further, possessed in addition, in a high degree, the power of awakening this knowledge in the inner life, so that it not only illuminates the external world, but also mediates for man that spiritual life, which from the profounder depths of his soul he needs must long after.

If we compare Nicholas with such spirits as Eckhart or Tauler, we obtain a remarkable result. Nicholas is the scientific thinker, striving to lift himself from research about the things of the world on to the level of a higher perception; Eckhart and Tauler are the faithful believers, who seek the higher life from within the content of this faith. Eventually

Nicholas arrives at the same inner life as Meister Eckhart; but the inner life of the former has a rich store of knowledge as its content.

The full significance of this difference becomes clear when we reflect that for the student of science the danger lies very near at hand of misunderstanding the scope of that species of knowing which enlightens us regarding the various special departments of knowledge. He can very readily be misled into believing that there really is only one single kind or mode of knowledge; and then he will either over- or under-rate this knowledge which leads us to the goal in the various special sciences. In the one case he will approach the subject-matter of the highest spiritual life as he would a problem in physics, and proceed to deal with it by means of concepts such as he would apply to gravitation or electricity. Thus, according as he believes himself to be more or less enlightened, the world will appear to him as a blindly working machine, or an organism, or as the teleological structure of a personal God: perhaps even as a form which is ruled and pervaded by a more or less clearly conceived "World-Soul." In the other case he notes that the knowledge, of which alone he has any experience, is adapted only to the things of the sense-world; and then he will become a sceptic, saying to himself: We can know nothing about things which lie beyond the world of the senses. Our knowledge has a limit. For the needs of the higher life we have no choice but to throw ourselves blindly into the arms of faith untouched by knowledge. And for a learned theologian like Nicholas of Cusa, who was also a scientist, this second danger lay peculiarly near at hand. For he emerged, along the lines of his learned training, from Scholasticism,—the way of conceiving things which was dominant in scientific life within the Mediæval Church; a mode of thought that St. Thomas Aquinas (1227-1274), the "Prince of Scholastics," had brought to its highest perfection. We must take this mode of conceiving things as the background, when we desire to portray the personality of Nicholas of Cusa.

Scholasticism is, in the highest degree, a product of human sagacity; and in it the logical capacity celebrated its highest triumphs. Any one who is striving to work out concepts in their sharpest, most clear-cut outlines, ought to go to the Scholastics for instruction. They afford us the High School for the technique of thinking. They possess an incomparable skill in moving in the field of pure thinking. It is easy to undervalue what they were able to achieve in this field; for it is only with difficulty accessible to man as regards most departments of knowledge. The majority rise to its level only in the domains of numbers and calculation, and in reflecting upon the connection of geometrical figures.

We can count by adding in thought a unity to a number, without needing to call to our help sense-conceptions. We calculate also, without such conceptions, in the pure element of thought. In regard to geometrical figures, we know that they never perfectly coincide with any sensible perception. There is no such thing within sensible reality as an "ideal" circle. Yet our thinking concerns itself with the purely ideal circle. For things and processes which are more complicated than forms of number and space, it is more difficult to find the ideal counterparts. This has even led so far that it has been contended, from various sides, that in the separated departments of knowledge there is only so much of real science as there is of measuring and counting.

The truth about this is that most men are not capable of grasping the pure thought-element where it is no longer concerned with what can be counted or measured. But the man who cannot do that for the higher realms of life and knowledge, resembles in that respect a child, which has not yet learned to count otherwise than by adding one pea to another. The thinker who said there was just so much real science in any domain as there was mathematics in it, was not very much at home in the matter. One ought rather to demand that everything which cannot be measured or counted should be handled just as ideally as the forms of number and space. And the Scholastics in the fullest way did justice to this demand. They sought everywhere the thought-content of things, just as the mathematician seeks it in the field of what is measurable and countable.

In spite of this perfected logical art, the Scholastics attained only to a one-sided and subordinate conception of Knowledge. Their conception is this: that in the act of knowing, man creates in himself an image of what he is to know. It is obvious, without further discussion, that with such a conception of the knowing process all reality must be located outside of the knowing. For one can grasp, in knowing, not the thing itself, but only an image of that thing.

Also, in knowing himself man cannot grasp himself, but again, what he does know of himself is only an image of himself. It is entirely from out of the spirit of Scholasticism that an accurate student thereof[*] says: "Man has in time no perception of his ego, of the hidden ground of his spiritual being and life, . . . he will never attain to beholding himself; for either, estranged for ever from God, he will find in himself only a fathomless, dark abyss, an endless emptiness, or else, made blessed in God, he will find on turning his gaze inwards just that very God, the sun of whose mercy is shining within him, whose image and likeness shapes itself in the spiritual traits of his nature."

Whoever thinks like this about all knowing, has only such a conception of knowing as is applicable to external things. The sensible factor in anything always remains external for us; therefore we can only take up into our knowledge pictures of whatever is sensible in the world. When we perceive a colour or a stone, we are unable, in order to know the being of the colour or the stone, to become ourselves the colour or the stone. Just as little can the colour or the stone transform itself into a part of our own being. It may, however, be questioned whether the conception of such a knowing-process, wholly directed to what is external in things, is an exhaustive one.

For Scholasticism, all human knowing does certainly in the main coincide with this kind of knowing. Another admirable authority on Scholasticism[†] characterises the conception of knowledge with which we are concerned in this direction of thought in the following manner: "Our spirit, allied in earth-life with the body, is primarily focussed upon the surrounding bodily world, but ordered in the direction of the spiritual therein: the beings, natures, forms of things, the elements of existence, which are related to our spirit and offer to it the rungs for its ascent to the super-sensuous; the field of our knowledge is therefore the realm of experience, but we must learn to understand what it offers, to penetrate to its meaning and thought, and thereby unlock for ourselves the world of thought."

The Scholastic could not attain to any other conception of knowledge, for the dogmatic content of his theology prevented his doing so. If he had directed the gaze of his spiritual eye upon that which he regards as an image only, he would then have seen that the spiritual content of

---

[*] K. Werner, in his book upon *Frank Suarez and the Scholasticism of the Last Centuries*, p. 122.
[†] Otto Willman, in his *History of Idealism*, vol. ii., p. 395.

things reveals itself in this supposed image; he would then have found that in his own inner being the God not alone images Himself, but that He lives therein, is present there in His own nature. He would have beheld in gazing into his own inner being, not a dark abyss, an endless emptiness, but also not merely an image of God; he would have felt that a life pulses within him, which is the very life of God itself; and that his own life is verily just God's life.

This the Scholastic dared not admit. The God must not, in his opinion, enter into him and speak forth from him; God must only be in him as an image. In reality, the Godhead must be external to the self. Accordingly, also, it could not reveal itself from within through the spiritual life, but must reveal itself from outside, through supernatural communication. What is aimed at in this, is just exactly what is least of all attained thereby. It is sought to attain to the highest possible conception of the Godhead. In reality, the Godhead is dragged down and made a thing among other things; only that these other things reveal themselves to us naturally, through experience; while the Godhead is supposed to reveal Itself to us supernaturally. A difference, however, between the knowledge of the divine and of the created is attained in this way: that as regards the created, the external thing is given in experience, so that we have knowledge of it; while as regards the divine, the object is not given to us in experience; we can reach it only in faith.

The highest things, therefore, are for the Scholastic not objects of knowledge, but mainly of faith. It is true that the relation of knowledge to faith must not be so conceived, according to the Scholastic view, as if in a certain domain only knowledge, and in another only faith reigned. For "the knowledge of that which is, is possible to us, because it, itself, springs from a creative element; things are for the spirit, because they are from the spirit; they have something to tell us, because they have a meaning which a higher intelligence has placed in them."* Because God has created the world according to thoughts, we too are able, when we grasp the thoughts of the world, to seize also upon the traces of the Divine in the world, through scientific reflection. But what God is, according to His own being, we can learn only from that revelation which He has given to us in supernatural ways, and in which we must believe. What we ought to think about the highest things, must be

---

* Otto Willman, *History of Idealism*, vol. ii., p. 383.

decided not by any human knowledge, but by faith; and "to faith belongs all that is contained in the writings of the New and of the Old Testament, and in the divine traditions."*

It is not our task here to present and establish in detail the relation of the content of faith to the content of knowledge. In truth, all and every faith-content originates from some actual inner human experience that has once been undergone. Such an experience is then preserved, as far as its outer form goes, without the consciousness of how it was acquired. And people maintain in regard to it that it came into the world by supernatural revelation. The content of the Christian faith was simply accepted by the Scholastics. Science, inner experience, had no business to claim any rights over it. As little as science can create a tree, just so little dared Scholasticism to create a conception of God; it was bound to accept the revealed one ready-made and complete, just as natural science has to accept the tree ready-made. That the spiritual itself can shine forth and live in man's inner nature, could never, never be admitted by the Scholastic. He therefore drew the frontier of the rightful power of knowledge at the point where the domain of outer experience ceases. Human knowledge must not dare to beget out of itself a conception of the higher beings; it is bound to accept a revealed one. The Scholastics naturally could not admit that in doing so they were accepting and proclaiming as "revealed" a conception which in truth had really been begotten at an earlier stage of man's spiritual life.

Thus, in the course of its development, all those ideas had vanished from Scholasticism which indicated the ways and means by which man had begotten, in a natural manner, his conceptions of the divine. In the first centuries of the development of Christianity, at the time of the Church Fathers, we see the doctrinal content of theology growing bit by bit by the assimilation of inner experiences. In Johannes Scotus Erigena, who stood at the summit of Christian theological culture in the ninth century, we find this doctrinal content being handled entirely as an inner living experience. With the Scholastics of the following centuries, this characteristic of an inner, living experience disappears altogether: the old doctrinal content becomes transposed into the content of an external, supernatural revelation.

One might, therefore, understand the activity of the mystical theolo-

---

* Joseph Kleutgen, *Die Theologie der Vorzeit*, vol. i., p. 39.

Eckhart, Tauler, Suso and their associates, in the following sense: they were stimulated by the doctrines of the Church, which were contained in its theology, but had been misinterpreted, to bring to birth afresh from within themselves, as inner living experience, a similar content.

Nicholas of Cusa sets out to mount from the knowledge one acquires in the isolated sciences up to the inner living experiences. There can be no doubt that the excellent logical technique which the Scholastics have developed, and for which Nicholas himself was educated, forms a most effective means of attaining to these inner experiences, even though the Scholastics themselves were held back from this road by their positive faith. But one can only understand Nicholas fully when one reflects that his calling as a priest, which raised him to the dignity of Cardinal, prevented him from coming to a complete breach with the faith of the Church, which found an expression appropriate to the age in Scholasticism. We find him so far along the road, that a single step further would necessarily have carried him out of the Church. We shall therefore understand the Cardinal best if we complete the one step more which he did not take; and then, looking backwards, throw light upon what he aimed at.

The most significant thought in Nicholas's mental life is that of "learned ignorance." By this he means a form of knowing which occupies a higher level as compared with ordinary knowledge. In the lower sense, knowledge is the grasping of an object by the mind, or spirit. The most important characteristic of knowing is that it gives us light about something outside of the spirit, that therefore it directs its gaze upon something different from itself. The spirit, therefore, is concerned in the knowing-process with things thought of as outside itself. Now what the spirit develops in itself about things is the being of those things. The things are spirit. Man sees the spirit so far only through the sensible encasement. What lies outside the spirit is only this sensible encasement; the being of the things enters into the spirit. If, then, the spirit turns its attention to this being of the things, which is of like nature with itself, then it can no longer talk of knowing; for it is not looking at anything outside of itself, but is looking at something which is part of itself; is, indeed, looking at itself. It no longer knows; it only looks upon itself. It is no longer concerned with a "knowing," but with a "not-knowing." No longer does man "grasp" something through the mind; he "beholds without conceiving" his own life. This highest stage of knowing is, in comparison with the lower stages, a "not-knowing."

But it is obvious that the essential being of things can only be reached through this stage of knowing. Thus Nicholas of Cusa in speaking of his "learned not-knowing" is really speaking of nothing else but "knowing" come to a new birth, as an inner experience. He tells us himself how he came to this inner experience. "I made many efforts to unite the ideas of God and the world, of Christ and the Church, into a single root-idea; but nothing satisfied me until at last, on my way back from Greece by sea, my mind's vision, as if by an illumination from above, soared up to that perception in which God appeared to me as the supreme Unity of all contradictions." To a greater or less extent this illumination was due to influences derived from the study of his predecessors. One recognises in his way of looking at things a peculiar revival of the views which we meet with in the writings of a certain Dionysius. The above-mentioned Scotus Erigena translated these writings into Latin, and speaks of their author as the "great and divine revealer."

The works in question are first mentioned in the first half of the sixth century. They were ascribed to that Dionysius, the Areopagite, named in the Acts of the Apostles, who was converted to Christianity by St. Paul. When these writings were really composed may here be left an open question. Their contents worked powerfully upon Nicholas as they had already worked upon Scotus Erigena, and as they must also have been in many ways stimulating for the way of thinking of Eckhart and his colleagues. This "learned not-knowing" is in a certain way preformed in these writings. Here we can only indicate the essential trait in the way of conceiving things found in these works. Man primarily knows the things of the sense-world. He forms thoughts about its being and action. The Primal Cause of all things must lie higher than these things themselves. Man therefore must not seek to grasp this Primal Cause by means of the same concepts and ideas as things. If he therefore ascribes to the Root-Being (God) attributes which he has learned to know in lower things, such attributes can be at best auxiliary conceptions of his weak spirit, which drags down the Root-Being to itself, in order to conceive it.

In truth, therefore, no attribute whatsoever which lower things possess can be predicated of God. It must not even be said that God "is." For "being" too is a concept which man has formed from lower things. But God is exalted above "being" and "not-being." The God to whom we ascribe attributes, is therefore not the true God. We come to the true God, when we think of an "Over-God" above and beyond any God with such attributes. Of this "Over-God" we can know nothing in the ordinary sense. In order to attain to Him, "knowing" must merge into "not-knowing."

One sees that at the root of such a view there lies the consciousness that man himself is able to develop a higher knowing, which is no longer mere knowing—in a purely natural manner—on the basis of what his various sciences have yielded him. The Scholastic view declared knowledge to be impotent to such a development; and, at the point where knowledge is supposed to cease, it called in to the help of knowledge a faith basing itself upon external revelation. Nicholas of Cusa was thus upon the road to develop out of knowledge itself that which the Scholastics had declared to be unattainable for knowledge.

We thus see that, from Nicholas of Cusa's point of view, there can be no question of there being only one kind or mode of knowing. On the contrary, for him, knowing clearly divides itself into two, first into such knowing as mediates our acquaintance with external objects, and second into such as is itself the object of which one gains knowledge. The first mode of knowing is dominant in the sciences, which teach us about the things and occurrences of the outer world; the second is in us when we ourselves live in the knowledge we have acquired. This second kind of knowing grows out of the first. Now, however, it is still one and the same world with which both these modes of knowing are concerned; and it is one and the self-same man who is active in both. Hence the question must arise, whence comes it that one and the self-same man develops two different kinds of knowledge of one and the same world.

Already, in connection with Tauler, the direction could be indicated in which the answer to this question must be sought. Here in Nicholas of Cusa this answer can be still more definitely formulated. In the first place, man lives as a separated (individual) being amidst other separated beings. In addition to the effects which the other beings produce on each other, there arises in his case the (lower) knowledge. Through his senses he receives impressions from other beings, and works up these impressions with his inner spiritual powers. He then turns his spiritual gaze away from external things, and beholds himself as well as his own activity. In so doing self-knowledge arises in him. But so long as he remains on this level of self-knowledge, he does not, in the true sense of the word, behold himself. He can still believe that some hidden being is active within him, whose manifestations and effects are *only* that which appears to him to be his own activities. But now the moment may come in which, through an incontrovertible inner experience, it becomes clear to the man that he experiences, in what he perceives or feels within himself, not the manifestation or effect of any hidden power or being, but this very being itself in its most essential and intimate form. Then he can say to himself: In a certain way I find all other things ready given, and I myself, standing apart from and outside of them, add to them whatever the spirit has to tell about them. But what I thus creatively add to the things in myself, therein do I myself live; that is myself, my very own being. But what is that which speaks there in the depths of my spirit? It is the knowledge which I have acquired of the things of the world. But in this knowledge there speaks no longer an effect, a manifestation; that which speaks expresses itself wholly, holding back nothing of what it contains. In this knowledge, there speaks the world in all its immediacy. But I have acquired this knowledge of things and of myself, as one thing among other things. From out my own being I myself speak, and the things, too, speak.

Thus, in truth, I am giving utterance no longer only to my own being; I am also giving utterance to the being of things themselves. My "ego" is the form, the organ in which the things express themselves about themselves. I have gained the experience that in myself I experience my own essential being; and this experience expands itself in me to the further one that in myself and through myself the All-Being Itself expresses Itself, or in other words, knows Itself. I can now no longer feel myself as a thing among other things; I can now only feel myself as a form in which the All-Being lives out Its own life.

It is thus only natural that one and the same man should have two modes of knowing. Judging by the facts of the senses, he is a thing among other things, and, in so far as he is that, he gains for himself a knowledge of these things; but at any moment he can acquire the higher experience that he is really the form in which the All-Being beholds Itself. Then man transforms himself from a thing among other things into a form of the All-Being—and, along with himself, the knowledge of things transforms itself into the expression of the very being of things. But as a matter of fact this transformation can only be accomplished through man. That which is mediated in the higher knowledge does not exist as long as this higher knowledge itself is not present. Man becomes only a real being in the creation of this higher knowledge; and only through man's higher knowledge can things also bring their being forth into real existence.

If, therefore, we demand that man shall add nothing to things through his inner knowledge, but merely give expression to whatever already exists in the things outside of himself, that would really amount to a complete abnegation of all higher knowledge. From the fact that man, in respect of his sensible life, is merely one thing among others, and that he only attains to the higher knowledge when he himself accomplishes with himself, as a being of the senses, the transformation into a higher being, it follows that he can never replace the one kind of knowledge by the other. His spiritual life consists, on the contrary, in a ceaseless oscillation between these two poles of knowledge—between knowing and seeing. If he shuts himself off from the seeing, he abandons the real nature of things: if he seeks to shut himself off from sense-perception, he would shut out from himself the things whose nature he seeks to know. It is these very same things which reveal themselves alike in the lower knowing and the higher seeing; only in the one case they reveal themselves according to their outer appearance; in the other according to their inner being. Thus it is not due to the things themselves that, at a certain stage, they appear only as external things; but their doing so is due to the fact that man must first of all raise and transform himself to the level upon which the things cease to be external and outside.

In the light of these considerations, some of the views which natural science has developed during the nineteenth century appear for the first time in the right light. The supporters of these views tell us that we hear, see, and touch the objects of the physical world through our senses. The eye, for instance, transmits to us a phenomenon of light, a colour. Thus we say that a body emits red light, when with the help of the eye we experience the sensation "red." But the eye can give us this same sensation in other cases also. If the eyeball is struck or pressed upon, or if an electric spark is allowed to pass through the head, the eye has a sensation of light.

It is thus evident that even in the cases in which we have the sensation of a body emitting red light, something may really be happening in that body which has no sort of resemblance to the colour we sensate. Whatever may be actually happening "outside of us" in space, so long as what happens is capable of making an impression on the eye, there arises in us the sensation of light. Thus what we experience *arises in us*, because we possess organs constituted in a particular manner. What happens outside in space, remains outside of us; we know only the effects which the external happenings call up in us. Hermann Helmholtz (1821-1893) has given a clearly outlined expression to this thought:

"Our sensations are simply effects which are produced in our organs by external causes, and the manner in which such an effect will show itself depends, naturally enough, altogether upon the kind of apparatus upon which the action takes place. In so far as the quality of our sensation gives us information as to the peculiar nature of the external action which produces the sensation, so far can the sensation be regarded as a sign or symbol of this external action, but not as an image or reproduction of it. For we expect in a picture some kind of resemblance to the object it represents; thus in a statue, resemblance of form; in a drawing, resemblance in the perspective projection of the field of view; in a painting, resemblance of colour in addition. A symbol, however, is not required to have any sort of resemblance to that which it symbolises. The necessary connection between the object and the symbol is limited to this: that the same object coming into action under the same conditions shall call up the same symbol, and that therefore different symbols shall always correspond to different objects. When berries of a certain kind in ripening produce together red colouration and sugar, then red colour and a sweet taste will always find themselves together in our sensation of berries of this form."*

Let us follow out step by step the line of thought which this view makes its own. It is assumed that something happens outside of me in

---

* Cp. Helmholtz, *Die Thatsachen der Wahrnehmung*, p. 12 *et seq.* I have characterised this kind of conception in detail in my *Philosophie der Freiheit*, Berlin, 1894, and in my *Welt- und Lebensanschauungen im Neunzehnten Jahrhundert*, vol. ii., p. i., etc.

space; this produces an effect upon my sense-organs; and my nervous system conducts the impression thus made to my brain. There another occurrence is brought about. I experience the sensation "red." Now follows the assertion: therefore the sensation "red" is not outside, not external to me; it is *in* me. All our sensations are merely symbols or signs of external occurrences of whose real quality we know nothing. We live and move in our sensations and know nothing of their origin. In the spirit of this line of thought, it would thus be possible to assert that if we had no eyes, colour would not exist; for then there would be nothing to translate this, to us, wholly unknown external happening into the sensation "red."

For many people this line of thought possesses a curious attraction; but nevertheless it originates in a complete misconception of the facts under consideration. (Were it not that many of the present day scientists and philosophers are blinded even to absurdity by this line of thought, one would need to say less about it. But, as a matter of fact, this blindness has ruined in many respects the thinking of the present day.) In truth, since man is but one object or thing among other things, it naturally follows that if he is to have any experience of them at all, they must make an impression upon him somehow or other. Something that happens outside the man must cause something to happen within him, if in his visual field the sensation "red" is to make its appearance.

The whole question turns upon this: What is without? what within? Outside of him something happens in space and time. But within there is undoubtedly a similar occurrence. For in the eye there occurs such a process, which manifests itself to the brain when I perceive the colour "red." This process which goes on "inside" me, I cannot perceive directly, any more than I can directly perceive the wave motions "outside" which the physicist conceives of as answering to the colour "red." But really it is only in this sense that I can speak of an "inside" and an "outside" at all. Only on the plane of sense-perception can the opposition between "outside" and "inside" hold good.

The recognition of this leads me to assume the existence "outside" of a process in space and time, although I do not directly perceive it at all. And the same recognition further leads me to postulate a similar process within myself, although I cannot directly perceive that either. But, as a matter of fact, I habitually postulate analogous occurrences in space and time in ordinary life which I do not directly perceive; as, for instance, when I hear piano-playing next door, and assume that a human being in space is seated at the piano and is playing upon it. And my conception, when I speak of processes happening outside of, and within me, is just the same. I assume that these processes have qualities analogous to those of the processes which do fall within the province of my senses, only that, because of certain reasons, they escape my direct perception.

If I were to attempt to deny to these processes all the qualities which my senses show me in the domains of space and time, I should in reality and in truth be trying to think something not unlike the famous knife without a handle, whose blade was wanting. Therefore, I can only say that space and time processes take place "outside" me; these bring about space and time processes "within" me; and both are necessary if the sensation "red" is to appear in my field of vision. And, in so far as this "red" is not in space and time, I shall seek for it equally in vain, whether I seek "without" or "within" myself. Those scientists and philosophers who cannot find it "outside," ought not to want to find it "inside" either. For it is not "inside," in exactly the same sense in which it is not "outside." To declare that the total content of that which the sense-world presents to us is but an inner world of sensation or feeling, and then to endeavour to tack on something "external" or "outside" to it, is a wholly impossible conception.

Hence, we must not speak of "red," "sweet," "hot," etc., as being symbols, or signs, which as such are only aroused within us, and to which "outside" of us something totally different corresponds. For that which is really set going within us, as the effect of some external happening, is something altogether other than what appears in the field of our sensations. If we want to call that which is within us a symbol, then we can say: These symbols make their appearance within our organism, in order to mediate to us the perceptions which, as such, in their immediacy, are neither within nor outside of us, but belong, on the contrary, to that common world, of which my "external" world and my "internal" world are only parts. In order to be able to grasp this common world, I must, it is true, raise myself to that higher plane of knowledge, for which an "inner" and an "outer" no longer exist. (I know quite well that people who pride themselves on the gospel that our entire world of experience builds itself up out of sensations and feelings of unknown origin will look contemptuously upon these remarks; as, for instance, Dr. Erich

Adikes in his book, *Kant contra Haeckel*, observes condescendingly: "At first people like Haeckel and thousands of his type philosophise gaily away without troubling themselves about theory of knowledge or critical self-reflection." Such gentlemen have no inkling of how cheap their own theories of knowledge are. They suspect the lack of critical self-reflection only in others. Let us leave to them their "wisdom.")

Nicholas of Cusa expresses some very telling thoughts bearing directly upon this very point. The clear and distinct way in which he holds apart the lower and the higher knowledge enables him, on the one side, to arrive at a full and complete recognition of the fact that man as a sense-being can only have in himself processes which, as effects, must necessarily be altogether unlike the corresponding external processes; while, on the other side, it guards him against confusing the inner processes with the facts which make their appearance in the field of our perceptions, and which, in their immediacy, are neither outside nor inside, but altogether transcend this opposition of "in" and "out."

But Nicholas was hampered in the thorough carrying through of these ideas by his "priestly garments." So we see how he makes a fine beginning with the progress from "knowing" to "not-knowing." At the same time we must also note that in the domain of the higher knowledge, or "ignorance," he unfolds practically nothing but the content of the theological teaching which the Scholastics also give us. Certainly he knows how to expound this theological content in a most able manner. He presents us with teachings about Providence, Christ, the creation of the world, man's salvation, the moral life, which are kept thoroughly in harmony with dogmatic Christianity. It would have been in accordance with his mental starting point, to say: I have confidence in human nature that after having plunged deeply into the science of things in all directions, it is capable of transforming from within itself this "knowing" into a "not-knowing," in such wise that the highest insight shall bring satisfaction. In that case, he would not simply have accepted the traditional ideas of the soul, immortality, salvation, God, creation, the Trinity, and so forth, as he actually did, but he would have represented his own.

But Nicholas personally was, however, so saturated with the conceptions of Christianity that he might well believe himself to have awakened in himself a "not-knowing" of his own, while yet he was merely bringing to light the traditional views in which he was brought up. But he stood upon the verge of a terrible precipice in the spiritual life of man. He was a *scientific* man. Now science, primarily, estranges us from the innocent harmony in which we live with the world so long as we abandon ourselves to a purely naïve attitude towards life. In such an attitude to life, we dimly feel our connection with the world-whole.

We are beings like others, forming links in the chain of Nature's workings. But with knowledge we separate ourselves off from this whole; we create within us a mental world, wherewith we stand alone and isolated over against Nature. We have become enriched; but our riches are a burden which we bear with difficulty; for it weighs primarily upon ourselves alone. And we must now, by our own strength, find the way back again to Nature. We have to recognise that we ourselves must now fit our wealth into the stream of world activities, just as previously Nature herself had fitted in our poverty. All evil demons lie in wait for man at this point. His strength can easily fail him. Instead of himself accomplishing this fitting in, he will, if his strength thus fails, seek refuge in some revelation coming from without, which frees him again from his loneliness, which leads back once more the knowledge that he feels a burden, into the very womb of being, into the Godhead. Like Nicholas of Cusa, he will believe that he is travelling his own road; and yet in reality he will be only following the path which his own spiritual evolution has pointed out for him.

Now there are—in the main—three roads which one can follow, when once one has reached the point at which Nicholas had arrived: the one is positive faith, forcing itself upon us from without; the second is despair; one stands alone with one's burden, and feels the whole universe tottering with oneself; the third road is the development of the deepest, most inward powers of man. Confidence, trust in the world must be one of our guides upon this third path; courage, to follow that confidence whithersoever it may lead us, must be the other.

AGRIPPA VON NETTESHEIM AND THEOPHRASTUS PARACELSUS

Both Heinrich Cornelius Agrippa von Nettesheim (1487-1535) and Theophrastus Paracelsus (1493-1541) followed the same road along which points Nicholas of Cusa's way of conceiving things. They devoted themselves to the study of Nature, and sought to discover her laws by all the means in their power and as thoroughly as possible. In this knowledge of Nature, they saw the true basis of all higher knowledge. They strove to develop this higher knowledge from within the science or knowledge of Nature by bringing that knowledge to a new birth in the spirit.

Agrippa von Nettesheim led a much varied life. He sprang from a noble family and was born in Cologne. He early studied medicine and law, and sought to obtain clear insight into the processes of Nature in the way which was then customary within certain circles and societies, or even among isolated investigators, who studiously kept secret whatever of the knowledge of Nature they discovered. For these purposes he went repeatedly to Paris, to Italy, and to England, and also visited the famous Abbot Trithemius of Sponheim in Würzburg. He taught at various times in learned institutions, and here and there entered the service of rich and distinguished people, at whose disposal he placed his abilities as a statesman and a man of science. If the services that he rendered are not always described by his biographers as unobjectionable, if it is said that he made money under the pretence of understanding secret arts and conferring benefits on people thereby, there stands against this his unmistakable, unresting impulse to acquire honestly the entire knowledge of his age, and to deepen this knowledge in the direction of a higher cognition of the world.

We may see in him very plainly the endeavour to attain to a clear and definite attitude towards natural science on the one hand, and to the higher knowledge on the other. But he only can attain to such an attitude who is possessed of a clear insight as to the respective roads which lead to one and to the other kind of knowledge. As true as it is on the one hand that natural science must eventually be raised into the region of the spirit, if it is to pass over into higher knowledge; so, also, it is true on the other, that this natural science must, to begin with, remain upon its own special ground, if it is to yield the right basis for the attainment of a higher level. The "spirit in Nature" exists only for spirit. So surely as Nature in this sense is spiritual, so surely too is there *nothing* in Nature, of all that is perceived by my bodily organs, which is immediately spiritual. There exists nothing spiritual which can appear to my eye as spiritual.

Therefore, I must not seek for the spirit as such in Nature; but that is what I am doing when I interpret any occurrence in the external world immediately as spiritual; when, for instance, I ascribe to a plant a soul which is supposed to be only remotely analogous to that of man. Further, I again do the same when I ascribe to spirit itself an existence in space and time; as, for instance, when I assert of the human soul that it continues to exist in time without the body, but yet after the manner of a body; or again, when I even go so far as to believe that, under any sort of conditions or arrangements perceivable by the senses, the spirit of a dead person can show itself.

Spiritualism, which makes this mistake, only shows thereby that it has not attained to a true conception of the spirit at all, but is still bent upon directly and immediately "seeing" the spirit in something grossly sensible. It mistakes equally both the real nature of the sensible and also that of the spirit. It de-spiritualises the ordinary world of sense, which hourly passes before our eyes, in order to give the name of spirit immediately to something rare, surprising, uncommon. It fails to understand that that which lives as the "spirit in nature" reveals itself to him who is able to perceive spirit in the collision of two elastic balls, for instance; and not only in occurrences which are striking from their rarity, and which cannot all at once be grasped in their natural sequence and connection.

But the spiritist further drags the spirit down into a lower sphere. Instead of explaining something that happens in space, and that he perceives through his senses only, in terms of forces and beings which in their turn are spacial and perceptible to the senses, he resorts to "spirits," which he thereby places exactly on a level with the things of the senses. At the very root of such a way of viewing things, there lies a lack of the power of spiritual apprehension. We are unable to perceive spiritual things spiritually; we therefore satisfy our craving for the spiritual with mere beings perceptible to the senses. Their own inner spirit reveals to such men nothing spiritual; and therefore they seek for the spiritual through the senses. As they see clouds flying through the air, so they would fain see spirits hastening along. Agrippa von Nettesheim fought for a genuine science of Nature, which shall explain the phenomena of Nature, not by means of spirits phenomenalising in the world of the senses, but by seeing in Nature only the natural, and in the spirit only the spiritual.

Of course, Agrippa will be entirely misunderstood if one compares *his* natural science with that of later centuries which dispose of wholly different experiences. In such a comparison, it might easily seem that he was still actually and entirely referring to the direct action of spirits, things which only depend upon natural connections or upon mistaken experience. Such a wrong is done to him by Moriz Carrière when he says, not in any malicious sense, it is true:

"Agrippa gives a huge list of things which belong to the Sun, the Moon, the Planets and the fixed stars, and receive influences from them; for instance: to the Sun are related Fire, Blood, Laurel, Gold, Chrysolite; they confer the gifts of the Sun: Courage, Cheerfulness, and Light. . . . Animals have a natural sense, which, higher than human understanding, approaches the spirit of prophecy. . . . Men can be bewitched to love and hate, to sickness and health. Thieves can be bewitched so that they cannot steal at some particular place, merchants, that they cannot do business, mills, that they cannot work, lightning flashes, that they cannot strike. This is brought about through drinks, salves, images, rings, incantations; the blood of hyenas or basilisks is adapted to such a purpose—it reminds one of Shakespeare's witches' cauldron." No; it does not remind one of that, if one understands Agrippa aright. He believed—it goes without saying—in many facts which in his time everybody regarded as unquestionable. But we still do the same to-day. Or do we imagine that future centuries will not relegate much of what we now regard as "undoubted fact" to the lumber-room of "blind" superstition?

I am convinced that in our knowledge of facts there has been a real progress. When once the "fact" that the earth is round had been discovered, all previous conjectures were banished into the domain of "superstition"; and the same holds good of certain truths of astronomy, biology, etc. The doctrine of natural evolution constitutes an advance, as compared with all previous "theories of creation," similar to that marked by the recognition of the roundness of the earth as contrasted with all previous speculations as to its form. Nevertheless, I am vividly conscious that in our learned scientific works and treatises there is to be found many a "fact" which will seem to future centuries to be just as little of a fact as much that Paracelsus and Agrippa maintain; but the really important point is not *what* they regarded as "fact," but *how*, in what spirit, they interpreted their "facts."

In Agrippa's time, there was little understanding or sympathy for the "natural magic" he represented, which sought in Nature the natural —the spiritual only in the spirit; men clung to the "supernatural magic," which sought the spiritual in the realm of the sensible, and which Agrippa combated. Therefore the Abbot Trithemius of Sponheim was right in giving him the advice to communicate his views only as a secret teaching to a few chosen pupils who could rise to a similar idea of Nature and spirit, because one "gives only hay to oxen and not sugar as to singing birds." It may be that Agrippa himself owed to this same Abbot his own correct point of view. In his *Steganography*, Trithemius has produced a book in which he handled with the most subtle irony that mode of conceiving things which confuses nature with spirit.

In this book he apparently speaks of nothing but supernatural occurrences. Any one reading it as it stands must believe that the author is talking of conjurations of spirits, of spirits flying through the air, and so on. If, however, one drops certain words and letters under the table, there remain—as Wolfgang Ernst Heidel proved in the year 1676— letters which, combined into words, describe purely natural occurrences. (In one case, for instance, in a formula of conjuration, one must drop the first and last words entirely, and then cancel from the remainder the second, fourth, sixth, and so on. In the words left over, one must again cancel the first, third, fifth letters and so on. One next combines what is then left into words; and the conjuration formula resolves itself into a purely natural communication.)

How difficult it was for Agrippa to work himself free from the prejudices of his time and to rise to a pure perception is proved by the fact that he did not allow his "Occult Philosophy" (*Philosophia Occulta*), already written in 1510, to appear before the year 1531, because he considered it unripe. Further evidence of this fact is given by his work "On the Vanity of the Sciences" (*De Vanitate Scientiarum*) in which he speaks with bitterness of the scientific and other activities of his time. He there states quite clearly that he has only with difficulty wrenched himself free from the phantasy which beholds in external actions immediate spiritual processes, in external facts prophetic indications of the future, and so forth.

Agrippa advances to the higher knowledge in three stages. He treats as the first stage the world as it is given for the senses, with its substances, its physical, chemical and other forces. He calls Nature, in so far as it is looked at on this level, "elementary Nature." On the second stage, one contemplates the world as a whole in its natural interconnection, as it orders things according to measure, number, weight, harmony, and so forth. The first stage proceeds from one thing to the next nearest. It seeks for the causes of an occurrence in its immediate surroundings. The second stage regards a single occurrence in connection with the entire universe. It carries through the idea that everything is subject to the influence of all other things in the entire world-whole. In its eyes this world-whole appears as a vast harmony, in which each individual item is a member. Agrippa terms the world, regarded from this point of view, the "astral" or "heavenly" world. The third stage of knowing is that wherein the spirit, by plunging deep into itself, perceives immediately the spiritual, the Root-Being of the world. Agrippa here speaks of the world, of soul and spirit.

The views which Agrippa develops about the world, and the relation of man to the world, present themselves to us in the case of Theophrastus Paracelsus, in a similar manner, only in more perfected form. It is better, therefore, to consider them in connection with the latter.

Paracelsus characterises himself aptly, when he writes under his portrait: "None shall be another's slave, who for himself can remain alone." His whole attitude towards knowledge is given in these words. He strives everywhere to go back himself to the deepest foundations of natural knowledge, in order to rise by his own strength to the loftiest regions of cognition. As Physician, he will not, like his contemporaries, simply accept what the ancient investigators, who then counted as authorities,—Galen or Avicenna, for instance, asserted long ago; he is resolved to read for himself directly in the book of Nature. "The Physician must pass Nature's examination, which is the world, and all its origins. And the very same that Nature teaches him, he must command to his wisdom, but seek for nothing in his wisdom, only and alone in the light of Nature." He shrinks from nothing, in order to learn to know Nature and her workings in all directions. For this purpose he made journeys to Sweden, Hungary, Spain, Portugal, and the East. He can truly say of himself: "I have followed the Art at the risk of my life, and have not been ashamed to learn from wanderers, executioners and sheep-shearers. My doctrine was tested more severely than silver in poverty, fears, wars and hardships."

What has been handed down by ancient authorities has for him no value, for he believes that he can attain to the right view only if he himself experiences the upward climb from the knowledge of Nature to the highest insight. This living, personal experience puts into his mouth the proud utterance: "He who will follow truth, must come into my monarchy. . . . After me; not I after you, Avicenna, Rhases, Galen, Mesur! After me; not I after you, O ye of Paris, ye of Montpellier, ye of Swabia, ye of Meissen, ye of Cologne, ye of Vienna and of what lies on the Danube and the Rhine; ye islands in the sea, thou Italy, thou Dalmatia, thou Athens, thou Greek, thou Arab, thou Israelite; after me, not I after you! Mine is the Monarchy."

It is easy to misunderstand Paracelsus because of his rough exterior, which sometimes conceals a deep earnestness behind a jest. Does he not himself say: "By nature I am not subtly woven, nor brought up on figs and wheat-bread, but on cheese, milk and rye-bread, wherefore I may well be rude with the over-clean and superfine; for those who were brought up in soft clothing and we who were bred in pine needles do not easily understand one another. When in myself I mean to be kindly,

I must therefore often be taken as rude. How can I not be strange to one who has never wandered in the sun?"

In his book about Winkelmann, Goethe has described the relation of man to Nature in the following beautiful sentence: "When the healthy nature of man acts as a whole; when he feels himself as one with a great, beautiful, noble and worthy whole; when the sense of harmonious well-being gives him a pure and free delight; then would the Universe, if it could be conscious of its own feeling, burst forth in joy at having attained its goal, and contemplate with wondering admiration the summit of its own becoming and being." With a feeling such as finds expression in these sentences, Paracelsus is simply saturated. From out of its depths the riddle of humanity takes shape for him. Let us watch how this happens in Paracelsus's sense.

At the outset, the road by which Nature has travelled to attain her loftiest altitude is hidden from man's power of comprehension. She has climbed, indeed, to the summit; but the summit does not proclaim: I feel myself as the whole of Nature; it proclaims, on the contrary: I feel myself as this single, separated human being. That which in reality is an achievement of the whole universe, feels itself as a separated, isolated being, standing alone by itself. This indeed is the true being of man, *viz.*, that he must needs feel himself to be something quite different from what, in ultimate analysis, he really is. And if that be a contradiction, then must man be called a contradiction come to life.

Man is the universe in his own particular way; he regards his oneness with the universe as a duality: he is the very same that the universe is; but he is the universe as a repetition, as a single being. This is the contrast which Paracelsus feels as the Microcosm (Man) and the Macrocosm (Universe). Man, for him, is the universe in miniature. That which makes man regard his relationship to the world in this way, that is his spirit. This spirit appears as if bound to a single being, to a single organism: and this organism belongs, by the very nature of its whole being, to the mighty stream of the universe. It is one member, one link in that whole, having its very existence only in relation with all the other links or members thereof. But spirit appears as an outcome of this single, separated organism, and sees itself at the outset as bound up only with that organism. It tears loose this organism from the mother earth out of which it has grown. So, for Paracelsus, a deep-seated connection between man and the universe lies hidden in the basic foundations of being, a connection which is hidden through the presence of "spirit." That spirit which leads us to higher insight by making knowledge possible, and leads on this knowledge to a new birth on a higher level—this has, as its first result for us men, to veil from us our own oneness with the whole.

Thus the nature of man resolves itself for Paracelsus in the first place into three factors: our sensuous-physical nature, our organism which appears to us as a natural being among other natural beings and is of like nature with all other natural beings; our concealed or hidden nature, which is a link in the chain of the whole universe, and therefore is not shut up within the organism or limited to it, but radiates and receives the workings of energy upon and from the entire universe; and our highest nature, our spirit, which lives its life in a purely spiritual manner. The first factor in man's nature Paracelsus calls the "elementary body"; the second, the ethereal-heavenly, or "astral body"; and the third he names "the Soul."

Thus in the "astral" phenomena, Paracelsus recognises an intermediate stage between the purely physical and the properly spiritual or soul-phenomena. Therefore these astral activities will come into view when the spirit or soul, which veils or conceals the natural basis of our being, suspends its activity. In the dream-world we see the simplest phenomena of this realm. The pictures which hover before us in dreams, with their remarkably significant connection with occurrences in our environment and with states of our inner nature, are products of our natural basis or root-being, which are obscured by the brighter light of the soul. For example, when a chair falls over beside my bed and I dream a whole drama ending with a shot fired in a duel; or when I have palpitation of the heart and dream of a boiling cauldron, we can see that in these dreams natural operations come to light which are full of sense and meaning, and disclose a life lying between the purely organic functions and the concept-forming activity which is carried on in the full, clear consciousness of the spirit. Connected with this region are all the phenomena belonging to the domain of hypnotism and suggestion; and in the latter are we not compelled to recognise an interaction between human beings, which points to some connection or relation between beings in Nature, which is normally hidden by the higher activity of the mind? From this starting point we can reach an understanding of what Paracelsus meant by the "astral" body. It is the sum total of those natural operations under whose influence we stand, or may in special circumstances come to stand, or which proceed from us, without our souls or minds coming into consideration in connection with them, but which yet cannot be included under the concept of purely physical phenomena. The fact that Paracelsus reckons as truths in this domain things which we doubt to-day, does not come into the question, from the point of view which I have already described.

Starting from the basis of these views as to the nature of man, Paracelsus divides him into seven factors or principles, which are the same as those we also find in the wisdom of the ancient Egyptians, among the Neoplatonists and in the Kabbalah. In the first place, man is a physical-bodily being, and therefore subject to the same laws as every other body. He is, in this respect, therefore, a purely "elementary" body. The purely physical-bodily laws combine into an organic life-process, and Paracelsus denotes this organic sequence of law by the terms "*archæus*" or "*spiritus vitæ*." Next, the organic rises into a region of phenomena resembling the spiritual, but which are not yet properly spiritual, and these he classifies as "astral" phenomena. From amidst these astral phenomena, the functions of the "animal soul" make their appearance. Man becomes a being of the senses.

Then he connects together his sense impressions according to their nature, by his understanding or mind, and the "human soul" or "reasoning soul" becomes alive in him. He sinks himself deep into his own mental productions, and learns to recognise "spirit" as such, and thus he has risen at length to the level of the "spiritual soul." Finally, he must come to recognise that in this spiritual soul he is experiencing the ultimate basis of universal being; the spiritual soul ceases to be individual, to be separated. Then arises the knowledge of which Eckhart spoke when he felt no longer that *he* was speaking within himself, but that in him the Root-Being was uttering Itself. The condition has come about in which the All-Spirit in man beholds Itself. Paracelsus has stamped the feeling of this condition with the simple words: "And that is a great thing whereon to dwell: there is naught in heaven or upon earth that is not in Man. And God who dwelleth in Heaven, He also is in Man."

With these seven principles of human nature, Paracelsus aims at expressing nothing else than the facts of inner and outer experience. The fact remains unquestioned that, what for human experience subdivides itself into a multiplicity of seven factors, is in higher reality a unity. But the higher insight exists just for the very purpose of exhibiting the unity in all that appears as multiplicity to man, owing to his bodily and spiritual organisation. On the level of the highest insight, Paracelsus strives to the utmost to fuse the unitary Root-Being of the world with his own spirit. But he knows that man can only cognise Nature in its spirituality, when he enters into immediate intercourse with that Nature. Man does not grasp Nature by peopling it from within himself with arbitrarily assumed entities; but by accepting and valuing it as it is, as Nature. Paracelsus therefore does not seek for God or for spirit in Nature; but Nature, just as it comes before his eyes, is for him wholly, immediately divine. Must one then first ascribe to the plant a soul after the kind of a human soul, in order to find the spiritual?

Hence Paracelsus explains to himself the development of things, so far as that is possible with the scientific means of his age, altogether in such wise that he conceives this development as a sensible-natural process. He makes all things to proceed from the root-matter, the root-water (Yliaster). And he regards as a further natural process the separation of the root-matter (which he also calls the great Limbus) into the four elements: Water, Earth, Fire and Air. When he says that the "Divine Word" called forth the multiplicity of beings from the root-matter, one must understand this also only in such wise as perhaps in more recent natural science one must understand the relationship of Force to Matter. A "Spirit," in a matter-of-fact sense, is not yet present at this stage. This "Spirit" is no matter-of-fact basis of the natural process, but a matter-of-fact result of that process.

This Spirit does not create Nature, but develops itself out of Nature. Not a few statements of Paracelsus might be interpreted in the opposite sense. Thus when he says: "There is nothing which does not possess and carry with it also a spirit hidden in it and that lives not withal. Also, not only has *that* life, which stirs itself and moves, as men, animals, the worms in the earth, the birds in the sky and the fishes in water, but all bodily and actual things as well."

But in such sayings Paracelsus only aims at warning us against that superficial contemplation of Nature which fancies it can exhaust the being of a thing with a couple of "stuck-up" concepts, according to Goethe's apt expression. He aims not at putting into things some imaginary being, but at setting in motion all the powers of man to bring out that which in actual fact lies in the thing.

What matters is not to let oneself be misled by the fact that Paracelsus expresses himself in the spirit of his time. It is far more important to recognise what things really hovered before his mind when, looking upon Nature, he expresses his ideas in the forms of expression proper to his age. He ascribes to man, for instance, a dual flesh, that is, a dual bodily constitution. "The flesh must also be understood, that it is of two kinds, namely the flesh that comes from Adam and the flesh which is not from Adam. The flesh from Adam is a gross flesh, for it is earthly and nothing besides flesh, that can be bound and grasped like wood and stone. The other flesh is not from Adam, it is a subtle flesh and cannot be bound or grasped, for it is not made of earth." What is the flesh that is from Adam? It is everything that man has received through natural development, everything, therefore, that has passed on to him by heredity. To that is added, whatever man has acquired for himself in his intercourse with the world around him in the course of time.

The modern scientific conceptions of inherited characteristics and those acquired by adaptation easily emerge from the above-cited thought of Paracelsus. The "more subtle flesh" that makes man capable of his intellectual activities, has not existed from the beginning in man. Man was "gross flesh" like the animal, a flesh that "can be bound and grasped like wood and stone." In a scientific sense, therefore, the soul is also an acquired characteristic of the "gross flesh." What the scientist of the nineteenth century has in his mind's eye when he speaks of the factors inherited from the animal world, is just what Paracelsus has in view when he uses the expression, "the flesh that comes from Adam."

Naturally I have not the least intention of blurring the difference that exists between a scientist of the sixteenth and one of the nineteenth century. It was, indeed, this latter century which for the first time was able to see, in the full scientific sense, the phenomena of living beings in such a connection that their natural relationship and actual descent, right up to man, stood out clearly before one's eyes. Science sees only a natural process where Linnæus in the eighteenth century saw a spiritual process and characterised it in the words: "There are counted as many species of living beings, as there were created different forms in the beginning." While thus in Linnæus's time, the Spirit had still to be transferred into the spacial world and have assigned to it the task of spiritually generating the forms of life, or "creating" them: the natural science of the nineteenth century could give to Nature what belonged to Nature, and to Spirit what belonged to Spirit. To Nature is even assigned the task of explaining her own creations; and the Spirit can plunge into itself there, where alone it is to be found, in the inner being of man.

But although in a certain sense Paracelsus thinks according to the spirit of his age, yet he has grasped the relationship of man to Nature in a profound manner, especially in relation to the idea of Evolution, of Becoming. He did not see in the Root-Being of the universe something which in any sense is there as a finished thing, but he grasped the Divine in the process of Becoming. Thereby he was enabled truly to ascribe to man a self-creative activity. For if the divine root of being is, as it were, given once for all, then there can be no question of any truly creative activity in man. It is not man, living in time, who then creates, but it is God, who is from Eternity, that creates. But for Paracelsus there is no such God from Eternity. For him there is only an eternal happening, and man is one link in this eternal happening. What man forms, was previously in no sense existent. What man creates, is, as he creates it, a new, original creation. If it is to be called divine, it can only be so-called in the sense in which it is a human creation. Therefore Paracelsus can assign to man a rôle in the building of the universe, which makes him a co-architect in its creation. The divine root of being is *without* man, not that which it is *with* man.

"For nature brings nothing to light, which as such is perfect, but man must make it perfect." This self-creative activity of man in the building of the universe is what Paracelsus calls Alchemy. "This perfecting is Alchemy. Thus the Alchemist is the baker, when he bakes bread, the vintager, when he makes wine, the weaver, when he makes cloth." Paracelsus aims at being an Alchemist in his own domain as a Physician. "Therefore I may well write so much here about Alchemy, that ye may well understand it, and experience that which it is and how it is to be understood; and not find a stumbling-block therein that neither Gold nor Silver shall come to thee therefrom. But have regard thereunto, that the Arcana [curative means] be revealed unto thee.... The third pillar of medicine is Alchemy, for the preparation of the medicines cannot come to pass without it, because Nature cannot be made use of without Art."

In the strictest sense, therefore, the eyes of Paracelsus are directed to

Nature, in order to overhear from herself what she has to say about that which she brings forth. He seeks to explore the laws of chemistry, so that, in his sense, he may work as an Alchemist. He pictures to himself all bodies as compounded out of three root-substances: Salt, Sulphur, and Mercury. What he thus names, naturally does not coincide with that which later chemistry solely and strictly calls by these names; just as little as that which Paracelsus conceives of as the root-substance is such in the sense of our later chemistry. Different things are called by the same names at different times. What the ancients called the four elements: Earth, Water, Air, and Fire, we still have to-day. But we call these four "elements" no longer "elements," but states of aggregation and have for them the designations: solid, liquid, gaseous and etheric. The Earth, for instance, was for the ancients not earth, but the "solid."

Again, we can clearly recognise the three root-substances of Paracelsus in contemporary conceptions, though not in present names of like sound. For Paracelsus, dissolution in a liquid and burning are the two most important chemical processes which he utilises. If a body be dissolved or burnt, it breaks up into its parts. Something remains behind as insoluble; something dissolves, or is burnt. What is left behind is to him of the nature of Salt; the soluble (liquid) of the nature of Mercury; while he terms Sulphur-like the part that can be burnt.

All this, taken as relating to material things, may leave the man cold who cannot look out beyond such natural processes; whoever seeks at all costs to grasp the spirit with his senses, will people these processes with all sorts of ensouling beings. He, however, who like Paracelsus knows how to regard them in connection with the whole, which permits its secret to become revealed in man's inner being,—he accepts them, as the senses offer them; he does not first re-interpret them; for just as the occurrences of Nature lie before us in their sensible reality, so too do they, in their own way, reveal to us the riddle of existence. That which through their sensible reality they have to unveil from within the soul of man, stands, for him who strives after the light of higher knowledge, far higher than all supernatural wonders that man can invent or get revealed to him about their suppositious "spirit." There is no "Spirit of Nature," capable of uttering loftier truths than the mighty works of Nature herself, when our soul links itself in friendship with that Nature and listens to the revelations of her secrets in intimate and tender intercourse. Such friendship with Nature was what Paracelsus sought.

VALENTINE WEIGEL AND JACOB BOEHME

In the view of Paracelsus, what mattered most was to acquire ideas about Nature which should breathe the spirit of the higher insight that he represented. A thinker related to him, who applied the same mode of conceiving things to his own nature especially, is VALENTINE WEIGEL (1533-1588). He grew up out of Protestant theology in a like sense to that in which Eckhart, Tauler, and Suso grew up out of Roman Catholic theology. He has predecessors in Sebastian Frank and Caspar Schwenckfeldt. These two, as contrasted with the orthodox Churchmen clinging to external profession, pointed downwards to the deepening of the inner life. For them it is not that Jesus whom the Gospels preach who is of value, but the Christ who can be born in every man as his deeper nature, and become for him the Saviour from the lower life and the guide to ideal uplifting.

Weigel performed silently and humbly the duties of his office as clergyman in Zschopau. It was only from the writings he left behind, printed first in the seventeenth century, that the world learned anything of the significant ideas which had come to him about the nature of man.*

---

* The following, from among his writings, may be named: *Der güldene Griff, das ist alle Ding ohne Irrthumb zu erkennen, vielen Hochgelehrten unbekandt, und doch allen Menschen nothwendig zu wissen; Erkenne dich selbst; Vom Ort der Welt.*

Weigel feels himself driven to gain a clear understanding of his relation to the teaching of the Church; and that leads him on further to investigate the basic foundations of all knowledge. Whether man can know anything through a confession of faith, is a question as to which he can only give himself an account when he knows *how* man knows. Weigel starts from the lowest kind of knowing. He asks himself: How do I know a sensible object, when it presents itself before me? Thence he hopes to be able to mount upwards to a point of view whence he can give himself an account of the highest knowledge.

In cognition through the senses, the instrument (the sense-organ) and the object, the "counterpart" (*Gegenwurf*) stand opposed. "Since in natural perception there must be two things, as the object or 'counterpart,' which is to be known and seen by the eye; and the eye, or the perceiver, which sees or knows the object, so do thou hold over against each other: whether the knowledge comes forth from the object to the eye; or whether the judgment, or the cognition, flows out from the eye into the object."* Weigel now says to himself: If the cognition (or knowledge) flowed from the "counterpart" (or thing) into the eye, then of necessity from one and the same thing a similar and perfect cognition must come to all eyes. But that is not the case, for each man sees according to the measure of his own eyes. Only the eyes, not the "counterpart" (or object) can be in fault, in that various and different conceptions are possible of one and the same thing. To clear up the matter, Weigel compares seeing with reading. If the book were not there, I naturally could not read it; but it might still be there, and yet I could read nothing in it, if I did not understand the art of reading. The book therefore must be there; but, from itself it can give me not the smallest thing; I must draw forth everything I read from within myself. That is also the nature of sensible perception. Colour is there as the "counterpart," but it can give the eye nothing from out of itself. The eye must recognise, from out of itself, what colour is. As little as the content of the book is in the reader, just so little is colour in the eye. If the content of the book were in the reader, he would not need to read it. Yet in reading, this content does not flow out from the book, but from the reader. So is it also with the sensible object. What the sensible thing before him is; that does not flow from outside into the man, but from within outwards.

---

* *Der güldene Griff*, p. 26 et seq.

Starting from these thoughts, one might say: If all knowledge flows out from man into the object, then one does not know what is in the object, but only what is in man. The detailed working out of this line of thought, brought about the view of Immanuel Kant (1724-1804).*

Weigel says to himself: Even if the knowledge flows out from man, it is still only the being of the "counterpart" (or object) which comes to light in this indirect way through man. As I learn the content of the book by reading it, and not by my own content, so also I learn the colour of the "counterpart" through the eye, not any colour to be found in the eye, or in myself. (Thus Weigel arrives by a road of his own at a result that we have already encountered in Nicholas of Cusa. Cp. pages 151-160). In this way Weigel attained to clearness as to the nature of sense-perception. He arrived at the conviction that everything which external things have to tell us can only flow forth from our own inner nature itself. Man cannot remain passive when he tries to know sensible objects and seeks merely to allow them to act upon him; but he must assume an active attitude, and bring forth the knowledge from within himself. The counterpart (or object) merely awakens the knowledge in the spirit. Man rises to higher knowledge when his spirit becomes its own "counterpart." One can see from sensible cognition that no cognition can flow into man from outside. Therefore there can be no such thing as an external revelation, but only an inner awakening.

As now the external counterpart waits till there comes into its presence man, in whom it can express its being, so too must man wait, when he seeks to be his own "counterpart" (or object) until the knowledge of his own being shall be awakened in him. If, in cognition through the senses, man must assume an active attitude in order that he may bring to meet the "counterpart" its own being, so in the higher knowing, man must hold himself passive, because he is himself now the "counterpart." He must admit its being into himself. Therefore the cognition of the spirit appears to him as enlightenment from above. In contrast to cognition through the senses, Weigel therefore terms the higher cognition the "Light of Mercy" This "Light of Mercy" is, in reality, nothing other

---

* The error in this line of thought will be found explained in my book, *The Philosophy of Freedom*, Berlin, 1894. Here I must limit myself to mentioning that Valentine Weigel, with his simple, robust way of conceiving things, stands far higher than Kant.

than the self-knowledge of the spirit in man, or the re-birth of knowledge on the higher level of beholding.

Now just as Nicholas of Cusa, in following up his road from knowing to beholding, does not really bring about the re-birth of the knowledge he has gained, on the higher level, but only the faith of the Church in which he was brought up appears deceptively before him as such a re-birth, so is it also the case with Weigel. He guides himself to the right road, but loses it again in the very moment in which he steps upon it. He who will travel the road that Weigel points out, can regard the latter as his guide only as far as the starting-point.

~

What rings out to meet us from the works of the Master-Shoemaker of Görlitz, JACOB BOEHME (1575-1624), sounds like the joyous outburst of Nature admiring her own being upon the summit of her evolution. A man appears before us whose words have wings, woven out of the inspiring feeling of having seen knowledge shining within him as Higher Wisdom. Jacob Boehme describes his own state as Piety which strives only to be Wisdom, and as a Wisdom that seeks to live only in Piety: "As I was wrestling and fighting in God's behalf, behold a wondrous light shone into my soul, such as was quite foreign to savage nature; therein I first knew what God and man were, and what God had to do with men."

Jacob Boehme no longer feels himself as a separated being expressing its insights; he feels himself as an organ of the great All-Spirit, speaking in him. The limits of his personality do not appear to him as the limits of the Spirit that speaks from within him. This Spirit is for him present everywhere. He knows that "the Sophist will blame him" when he speaks of the beginning of the world and its creation: "the while I was not thereby and did not myself see it. To him be it said that in the essence of my soul and body, when I was not yet the 'I,' but when I was still Adam's essence, I was there present and myself squandered away my glory in Adam."

Only in external similes is Boehme able to indicate how the light broke forth in his inner being. When once as a boy he finds himself on the top of a mountain, he sees above him a place where large red stones seem to shut up the mountain; the entrance is open and in its depth he sees a vessel full of gold. A shudder runs through him; and he goes on his way without touching the treasure. Later on he is apprenticed to a shoemaker in Görlitz. A stranger steps into the shop and demands a pair of shoes. Boehme is not allowed to sell them in the absence of his master. The stranger departs, but after a while calls the apprentice out of the shop and says to him: "Jacob, thou art little, but thou wilt some day become quite another man, over whom the world will break out into wonder." In riper years, Jacob Boehme sees the reflection of the bright sun in a tin vessel: the view that thus presents itself to him seems to him to unveil a profound secret. Even after the impression of this appearance, he believes himself to be in possession of the key to the riddles of Nature.

He lives as a spiritual anchorite, humbly earning his living by his trade, and between whiles, as though for his own recollection, he notes down the harmonies which resound in his inner being when he feels the Spirit in himself. The zealotry of priestly fervour makes life hard for the man; he, who desires naught but to read the Scripture which the light of his inner nature illuminates for him, is persecuted and tortured by those to whom only the external writ, the rigid, dogmatic confession of faith, is accessible.

One world-riddle remains as a disquieting presence in Jacob Boehme's soul, driving him on to knowledge. He believes himself to be in his spirit enfolded in a divine harmony; but when he looks around him, he sees discord everywhere in the divine workings. To man belongs the light of Wisdom; and yet he is exposed to error; in him lives the impulse to the good, and yet the discord of evil sounds throughout the whole of human development. Nature is governed by its own great laws; yet its harmony is disturbed by happenings of no purport, and the warfare of the elements. How is this discord in the harmonious world-whole to be understood? This question tortures Jacob Boehme. It strides into the centre of the world of his thought. He strives to gain a view of the world as a whole, which shall include the discordant. For how can a conception which leaves the actual present discord unexplained explain the world? The discord must be explained out of the harmony, the evil out of the good itself. Let us restrict ourselves, in speaking of these things, to the good and the evil, wherein the lack of harmony in the narrower sense finds its expression. For, fundamentally, Jacob Boehme also restricts himself to this. He can do so, for Nature and man appear to him as a single entity. He sees in both similar laws and processes. The purposeless seems to him an evil something in Nature, just as evil seems to him something purposeless in man. Similar fundamental forces rule both here and there. To one who has known the origin of evil in man, the source of evil in Nature also lies open and clear.

Now, how can the evil as well as the good flow forth from the very same Root-Being? Speaking in Jacob Boehme's sense, one would give the following answer. The Root-Being does not live out its existence in itself. The multiplicity of the world shares in this existence. As the human body lives its life, not as a single member, but as a multiplicity of members, so also the Root-Being. And as human life is poured out into this multiplicity of members, so too the Root-Being is poured out into the manifoldness of the things of this world. As true as it is that the entire man has only one life, so true is it that every member has its own life. And as little as it contradicts the whole harmonious life of a man, that his hand should turn itself against his own body and wound it, so little is it impossible that the things of the world, which live the life of the Root-Being in their own way, should turn themselves against each other. Thus the Root-Being, in dividing itself among different lives, confers upon each such life the capacity to turn itself against the whole.

It is not from the good that evil streams forth, but from the way in which the good lives. As the light is only able to shine when it pierces the darkness, so the good can bring itself to life only when it permeates its opposite. From out of the "fathomless abyss" of darkness there streams forth the light; from the "groundlessness" of the indifferent there is brought to birth the Good. And as in the shadow only the brightening demands a pointing to the light; but the darkness, as a matter of course, is felt as that which weakens the light; so too in the world, it is only the law-abiding character that is sought for in all things; and the evil, the purposeless, is accepted as a matter of course, intelligible in itself. Thus, in spite of the fact that for Jacob Boehme the Root-Being is the All, still nothing in the world can be understood, unless one has an eye both to the Root-Being and its opposite at once. "The good has swallowed up into itself the evil or the hideous. . . . Every being has in itself good and evil, and in its unfoldment, as it passes over into division, it becomes a contradiction of qualities, as one seeks to overcome the other."

Hence it is altogether in accordance with Jacob Boehme's view to see in everything, and in every process of the world, both good and evil; but it is not in accord with his meaning, without more ado to seek the Root-Being in the mingling of good and evil. The Root-Being must swallow up the evil; but the evil is not a part of the Root-Being. Jacob Boehme seeks the Root-Being of the world; but the world itself has sprung forth from the "fathomless abyss" through the Root-Being. "The external world is not God, and eternally will not be called God, but only a being wherein God manifests Himself. . . . When one says: God is all, God is heaven and earth, and also the outer world, so is that true: for from him and in him all stands originally rooted. But what am I to do with such a saying, which is no religion?"

With such a view in the background, Jacob Boehme's conceptions as to the being of the whole world built themselves up in his mind, so that he makes the orderly world emerge in a series of steps from the "fathomless abyss." This world builds itself up in seven natural forms. In dark astringency the Root-Being receives form, dumbly shut up within itself and motionless. This astringency Boehme grasps under the symbol of Salt. In employing such designations he leans upon Paracelsus, who had borrowed from chemical processes his names for the processes of Nature. By swallowing up its opposite, the first nature-form passes over into the form of the second; the astringent, the motionless, takes on movement; Power and Life enter into it. Quicksilver (Mercury) is the symbol for this second form. In the struggle of Rest and Motion, of Death with Life, the third form of Nature unveils itself (Sulphur). This Life battling within itself, becomes manifest to itself; it lives thenceforward no longer an outer battle of its members; there quivers through it as it were a unifying glowing flash, itself lighting up its own being (Fire). This fourth form of Nature rises to the fifth, the living battle of the parts resting in themselves (Water). On this level, as upon the first, there is present an inner astringency and dumbness; only it is not an absolute rest, a silence of the inner opposites, but an interior movement of the opposites. It is not the motionless resting in itself, but the moved, that which has been kindled by the fire-flash of the fourth stage. Upon the sixth level, the Root-Being itself becomes aware of itself as such inner life. Living beings endowed with senses represent this form of Nature. Jacob Boehme calls it the "Clang" or Call, and in so doing adopts the sense-perception of sound as the symbol for sense-perception in general. The seventh form of Nature is the Spirit, raising itself on the basis of its sense-perceptions (Wisdom). He finds himself again as himself, as the Root-Being, within the world that has grown up out of the "fathomless abyss," shaping itself out of the harmonious and the discordant. "The Holy Ghost brings the Glory of this Majesty into the being, wherein the Godhead stands revealed."

It is with such views that Jacob Boehme seeks to fathom that world which for him, according to the knowledge of his time, was reckoned as the actual world of fact. For him all is fact which is so regarded by the natural science of his time and by the Bible. His way of conceiving things is one thing, his world of facts quite another. One can imagine the former applied to a totally different knowledge of facts. And thus there appears before our eyes a Jacob Boehme as he might stand at the parting of the nineteenth and the twentieth centuries. Such a one would not saturate with his way of conceiving things the six days' creation work of the Bible and the fight of the angels and the devils, but Lyell's geological knowledge and the facts of Haeckel's *The History of Creation*. He who can penetrate into the spirit of Jacob Boehme's writings must arrive at this conviction.*

---

* We may here name the most important of Boehme's writings: *Die Morgenröthe im Aufgang; Die drei Prinzipien göttlichen Lebens oder über das dreifache Leben des Menschen; Das umgewandte Auge; "Signatura rerum" oder von der Geburt und Bezeichnung aller Wesen; Das "Mysterium Magnum."*

GIORDANO BRUNO AND ANGELUS SILESIUS

In the first decennium of the sixteenth century, the scientific genius of Nicholas Copernicus (1473-1543) thinks out in the castle of Heilsberg, in Prussia, an intellectual structure which compels the men of subsequent epochs to look up to the starry heavens with other conceptions than those which their forefathers in antiquity and the Middle Ages had. To them the earth was their dwelling-place, at rest in the centre of the Universe. The stars, however, were for them beings of a perfect nature, whose motion took place in circles because the circle is the representative of perfection.

In that which the stars showed to human senses they beheld something of the nature of soul, something spiritual. It was one kind of speech that the things and processes upon earth spoke to man; quite another, that of the shining stars, beyond the moon in the pure æther, which seemed like some spiritual nature filling space. Nicholas of Cusa had already formed other ideas.

Through Copernicus, earth became for man a brother-being in face of the other heavenly bodies, a star moving like others. All the difference that earth has to show for man he could now reduce to this: that earth is his dwelling-place. He was no longer forced to think differently about the events of this earth and those of the rest of universal space. The world of his senses had expanded itself into the most remote spaces. He was compelled henceforth to allow that which penetrated his eye from the æther to count as sense-world just as much as the things of earth. He could no longer seek in the æther in sensuous fashion for the Spirit.

Whoever, henceforth, strove after higher knowledge, must needs come to an understanding with this expanded world of the senses. In earlier centuries, the brooding mind of man stood before a world of facts. Now he was confronted with a new task. No longer could the things of earth only express this nature from within man's inner being. This inner nature of his was called on to embrace the spirit of a sense-world, which fills the All of Space everywhere alike.

The thinker of Nola, PHILOTHEO GIORDANO BRUNO (1548-1600) found himself faced by such a problem. The senses have conquered the universe of space; henceforth the Spirit is no more to be found in space. Thus man was guided from without to seek henceforward for the Spirit there alone where from out of profound inner experiences those glorious thinkers sought it, whose ranks our previous expositions have led before us. These thinkers drew upon a view of the world to which, later on, the advance of natural knowledge forces humanity. The sun of those ideas, which later should shine upon a new view of Nature, with them still stands below the horizon; but their light already appears as the early dawn at a time when men's thoughts of Nature itself still lay in the darkness of night.

The sixteenth century gave the heavenly spaces to natural science for the sense-world to which it rightfully belongs; by the end of the nineteenth century, this science had advanced so far that, even within the phenomena of plant, animal, and human life, it could assign to the world of sensible facts that which belongs to it. Neither, then, in the æther above, nor in the development of living creatures, can this natural science henceforth seek for anything but sensible, matter-of-fact processes. As the thinker in the sixteenth century had to say: "The earth is a star among other stars, subject to the same laws as other stars"; so must the thinker of the nineteenth century say: "Man, whatever may be his origin and his future, is for anthropology only a mammal, and further, that mammal whose organisation, needs and diseases are the most complex, whose brain, with its marvellous capacities, has reached the highest level of development."*

From such a standpoint, attained through natural science, there can

---

* Paul Topinard: *Anthropologie*, Leipzig, 1888, p. 528.

no longer occur any confusion between the spiritual and the sensible, provided man understands himself rightly. Developed natural science makes it impossible to seek in Nature for a Spirit conceived of after the fashion of something material, just as healthy thinking makes it impossible to seek for the reason of the forward movement of the clock-hand, not in mechanical laws (the Spirit of inorganic Nature), but in a special Daimon, supposed to bring about the movements of the hands. Ernst Haeckel was quite right in rejecting, as a scientist, the gross conception of a God conceived of in material fashion. "In the higher and more abstract forms of religion, the bodily appearance is abandoned and God is worshipped as pure Spirit, devoid of body. 'God is a Spirit, and they that worship him must worship him in spirit and in truth.' But, nevertheless, the soul-activity of this pure Spirit remains quite the same as that of the anthropomorphic personal God. In reality, even this immaterial Spirit is not thought of as bodiless, but as invisible, like a gas. We thus arrive at the paradoxical conception of God as a gaseous vertebrate."*

In reality, the matter-of-fact, sensible existence of something spiritual may be assumed only when immediate sensible experience shows something spiritual, and only such a degree of the spiritual may be assumed as can be perceived in this manner. That first rate thinker, B. Carneri, ventured to say (in his book: *Empfindung und Bewusstsein*, p. 15): "The dictum: No spirit without matter, but also no matter without spirit,—would entitle us to extend the question to the plant also, nay, even to any block of stone taken at random, wherein there seems very little to speak in favour of these correlative conceptions." Spiritual occurrences as matters of fact are the results of various doings of an organism; the Spirit of the world is not present in the world in a material sense, but precisely after a spiritual fashion. Man's soul is a sum of processes in which Spirit appears most immediately as fact. In the form of such a soul, however, Spirit is present in man only. And it implies that one misunderstands Spirit, that one commits the worst sin against Spirit, to seek for Spirit in the form of Soul elsewhere than in man, to imagine other beings thus ensouled as man is. Whoever does this, only shows that he has not experienced Spirit within himself; he has only experienced that outer form of appearance of Spirit, the Soul, which

---

* Haeckel, *Riddle of the Universe*.

reigns in him. But that is just the same as though one regarded a circle drawn with a pencil as the real, mathematically ideal circle. Whoever experiences in himself nothing other than the soul-form of the Spirit, feels himself thereupon driven to assume also such a soul-form in non-human things, in order that thereby he may not need to remain rooted in the materiality of the gross senses. Instead of thinking the Root-Being of the world as Spirit, he thinks of it as World-Soul, and postulates a general ensoulment of Nature.

Giordano Bruno, upon whom the new Copernican view of Nature forced itself, could grasp Spirit in the world, from which it had been expelled in its old form, in no other manner than as World-Soul. On plunging into Bruno's writings (especially his deeply thoughtful book: *De Rerum Principiis et Elementis et Causis*) one gets the impression that he thought of things as ensouled, although in varying degree. He has not, in reality, experienced in himself the Spirit, therefore he conceives Spirit after the fashion of the human soul, wherein alone he has encountered it. When he speaks of Spirit, he conceives of it in the following way: "The universal reason is the inmost, most effective and most special capacity, and a potential part of the World-Soul; it is something one and identical, which fills the All, illuminates the universe and instructs Nature how to bring forth her species as they ought to be." In these sentences Spirit, it is true, is not described as a "gaseous vertebrate," but it is described as a being that is like to the human soul. "Let now a thing be as small and tiny as you please, it yet has within it a portion of spiritual substance, which, when it finds a substratum adapted thereto, reaches out to become a plant, an animal, and organises itself to any body you choose that is ordinarily called ensouled. For Spirit is to be found in all things, and there does not exist even the tiniest little body which does not embrace in itself such a share thereof as causes it to come to life."

Because Giordano Bruno had not really experienced the Spirit, as Spirit, in himself, he could therefore confuse the life of the Spirit with the external mechanical processes, wherewith Raymond Lully (1235-1315) wanted to unveil the secrets of the Spirit in his so-called "Great Art" (*Ars Magna*). A recent philosopher, Franz Brentano, describes this "Great Art" thus: "Concepts were to be inscribed upon concentric, separately revolving discs, and then the most varied combinations produced by turning them about." Whatever chance brings up in the turning of these discs, was shaped into a judgment about the highest truths. And Giordano Bruno, in his manifold wanderings through Europe, made his appearance at various seats of learning as a teacher of this "Great Art." He possessed the daring courage to think of the stars as worlds, perfectly analogous to our earth; he widened the outlook of scientific thinking beyond the confines of earth; he thought of the heavenly bodies no longer as bodily spirits; but he still thought of them as soul-like spirits. One must not be unjust towards the man whom the Catholic Church caused to pay with death the penalty for his advanced way of thinking. It required something gigantic to harness the whole space of heaven in the same view of the universe which hitherto had been applied only to things upon earth, even though Bruno did still think of the sensible as soul-like.

~

In the seventeenth century there appeared Johann Scheffler, called ANGELUS SILESIUS (1624-1677), a personality in whom there once more shone forth, in mighty harmony of soul, what Tauler, Weigel, Jacob Boehme, and others, had prepared. Gathered, as it were, into a spiritual focus and shining with enhanced light-giving power, the ideas of the thinkers named make their appearance in his book: "Cherubinischer Wandersmann. Geistreiche Sinn- und Schlussreime." And everything that Angelus Silesius utters appears as such an immediate, inevitable, natural revelation of his personality, that it is as though this man had been called by a special providence to embody wisdom in a personal form. The simple, matter-of-course way in which he lives wisdom, attains its expression by being set forth in sayings which, even in respect of their art and their form, are worthy of admiration. He hovers like some spiritual being over all earthly existence; and what he says is like the breath of another world, freed beforehand from all that is gross and impure, wherefrom human wisdom generally only toilsomely works itself free.

He only is truly a knower, in the sense of Angelus Silesius, who brings the eye of the All to vision in himself; he alone sees his action in the true light who feels that this action is wrought in him by the hand of the All: "God is in me the fire, and I in him the light; are we not in most intimate communion one with another?"—"I am as rich as God; there can be no grain of dust that I—believe me, man,—have not in common with Him."—"God loves me above Himself; if I love Him above myself: I so give Him as much as He gives me from Himself."—"The bird flies in the air, the stone rests on the earth; in water lives the fish, my spirit in God's own hand."—"Art thou born of God, then bloometh God in thee; and His Godhead is thy sap and thy adornment."—"Halt! whither runnest thou? Heaven is in thee: seekest thou God otherwhere, thou missest Him ever and ever."

For one who thus feels himself in the All, every separation ceases between self and another being; he no longer feels himself as a single individual; rather does he feel all that there is of him as a part of the world, his own proper being, indeed, as that World-Whole itself. "The world, it holds thee not; thou art thyself the world that holds thee, in thee, with thee, so strongly captive bound."—"Man has never perfect bliss before that unity has swallowed up other-ness."—"Man is all things; if aught is lacking to him, then in truth he knoweth not his own riches."

As a sense-being, man is a thing among other things, and his sense-organs bring to him, as a sensible individuality, sense-news of the things in space and time outside of him; but when Spirit speaks in man, then there remains no without and no within; nothing is here and nothing is there that is spiritual; nothing is earlier and nothing is later; space and time have vanished in the contemplation of the All-Spirit. Only so long as man looks forth as an individual, is he here and the thing there; and only so long as he looks forth as an individual, is this earlier, and this later. "Man, if thou swingest thy spirit over time and place, so each moment canst thou be in eternity."—"I am myself eternity when I leave time behind, and self in God and God in self together grasp."—"The rose that here thine outer eye doth see, it so hath bloomed in God from all eternity."—"In centre set thyself, so see'st thou all at once: what then and now occurred, here and in heaven's realm."—"So long for thee, my friend, in mind lies place and time: so long graspest thou not what's God, nor what eternity."—"When man from manifoldness withdraws, and inward turns to God, so cometh he to unity." The summit has thus been climbed, whereon man steps forth beyond his individual "I" and abolishes every opposition between the world and himself. A higher life begins for him. The inner experience that comes over him appears to him as the death of the old and a resurrection in a new life. "When thou dost raise thyself above thyself and lettest God o'errule; then in thy spirit happens ascension into heaven."—"The body in the spirit must arise, the spirit, too, in God: if thou in him, my man, will live for ever blessed."—"So much mine 'I' in me doth 'minish and decrease; so much therefore to power cometh the Lord's own 'I.'"

From such a point of view, man recognises his meaning and the meaning of all things in the realm of eternal necessity. The natural All appears to him immediately as the Divine Spirit. The thought of a divine All-Spirit, who could still have being and sub-existence over and beside the things of the world, vanishes away as a superseded conception. This All-Spirit appears so outpoured into things, so becomes one in being with the things, that it could no longer be thought at all, if even one single member were thought away from its being. "Naught is but I and thou; and if we twain were not; then is God no more God, and heaven falleth in."—Man feels himself as a necessary link in the world-chain. His doing has no longer aught of arbitrariness or of individuality in it. What he does is necessary in the whole, in the world-chain, which would fall to pieces if this his doing were to fall out from it. "God may not make without me a single little worm: if I with him uphold it not, straightway must it burst asunder."—"I know that without me God can no moment live: if I come to naught, he needs must give up the ghost." —Upon this height, man for the first time sees things in their real being. He no longer needs to ascribe from outside to the smallest thing, to the grossly sensible, a spiritual entity. For just as this minutest thing is, in all its smallness and gross sensibility, it is a link in the Whole. "No grain of dust is so vile, no mote can be so small: the wise man seeth God most gloriously therein."—"In a mustard seed, if thou wilt understand it, is the image of all things above and beneath."

Man feels himself free upon this height. For constraint is there only where a thing can constrain from without. But when all that is without has flowed into the within, when the opposition between "I and world," "Without and Within," "Nature and Spirit," has disappeared, man then feels all that impels him as his own impulse. "Shut me, as strongly as thou wilt, in a thousand irons: I still will be quite free and unfettered." —"So far as my will is dead, so far must God do what I will; I myself prescribe to him the pattern and the goal."—At this point cease all moral obligations, coming from without: man becomes to himself measure and goal. He is subject to no law; for the law, too, has become his being. "For the wicked is the law; were there no command written, still would the pious love God and their neighbour."

Thus, on the higher level of knowledge, the innocence of Nature is given back to man. He fulfils the tasks that are set him in the feeling of an external necessity. He says to himself: Through this iron necessity it is given into thy hand to withdraw from this very iron necessity the link which has been allotted to thee. "Ye men, learn but from the meadow flower: how ye shall please God and be beautiful as well."—"The rose exists without why and because, she blooms because she blooms; she takes no heed of herself, asks not if men see her." The man who has arisen upon the higher level feels in himself the eternal, necessary pressure of the All, as does the meadow flower; he acts, as the meadow flower blooms. The feeling of his moral responsibility grows in all his doing into the immeasurable. For that which he does not do is withdrawn from the All, is a slaying of that All, so far as the possibility of such a slaying lies with him. "What is it, not to sin? Thou need'st not question long: go, the dumb flowers will tell it thee."—"All must be slain. If thou slayest not thyself for God, then at last eternal death shall slay thee for the enemy."

AFTERWORD

Nearly two and a half centuries have passed since Angelus Silesius gathered up the profound wisdom of his predecessors in his *Cherubinean Wanderer*. These centuries have brought rich insights into Nature. Goethe opened a vast perspective to natural science. He sought to follow up the eternal, unchangeable laws of Nature's working, to that summit where, with like necessity, they cause man to come into being, just as on a lower level they bring forth the stone.* Lamarck, Darwin, Haeckel, and others, have laboured further in the direction of this way of conceiving things. The "question of all questions," that in regard to the natural origin of man, found its answer in the nineteenth century; and other related problems in the realm of natural events have also found their solutions. To-day men comprehend that it is not necessary to step outside of the realm of the actual and the sensible in order to understand the serial succession of beings, right up to man, in its development in a purely natural manner.

And, further, J. G. Fichte's penetration has thrown light into the being of the human ego, and shown the soul of man where to seek itself and what it is.† Hegel has extended the realm of thought over all the

---

* Cp. my book: *Goethe's Weltanschauung*, Weimar, 1897.
† Cp. ante, and the section upon Fichte in my book: *Welt- und Lebensanschauungen im neunzehnten Jahrhundert*, vol. i., Berlin, S. Cronbach.

provinces of being, and striven to grasp in thought the entire sensible existence of Nature, as also the loftiest creations of the human spirit.*

How, then, do those men of genius whose thoughts have been traced in the preceding pages, appear in the light of a world-conception which takes into account the scientific achievements of the centuries that followed their epoch? They still believed in a "supernatural" story of creation. How do their thoughts appear when confronted with a "natural" history of creation, which the science of the nineteenth century has built up?

This natural science has given to Nature naught that did not belong to her; it has only taken from her what did not belong to her. It has banished from Nature all that is not to be sought in her, but is to be found only in man's inner being. It sees no longer any being in Nature that is like unto the human soul, and that creates after the manner of man. It no longer makes the organic forms to be created by a man-like God; it follows up their development in the sense-world according to purely natural laws. Meister Eckhart, as well as Tauler, and also Jacob Boehme with Angelus Silesius, would needs feel the deepest satisfaction in contemplating this natural science. The spirit in which they desired to behold the world has passed over in the fullest sense to this view of Nature, when it is rightly understood. What they were still unable to do, *viz.*: to bring the facts of Nature themselves into the light which had risen for them, that, undoubtedly, would have been their longing, if this same natural science had been laid before them. They could not do it; for no geology, no "natural history of creation" told them about the processes in Nature. The Bible alone told them in its own way about such processes. Therefore they sought, so far as they could, for the spiritual where alone it is to be found: in the inner nature of man.

At the present time, they would have quite other aids at hand than in their own time, to show that an actually existing Spirit is to be found only in man. They would to-day agree unreservedly with those who seek Spirit as a fact not in the root of Nature, but in her fruit. They would admit that Spirit as perceivable is a result of evolution, and that upon lower levels of evolution such Spirit must not be sought for. They would understand that no "creative thought" ruled in the forthcoming

---

* Cp. my presentation of Hegel in *Welt- und Lebensanschauungen im neunzehnten Jahrhundert*, vol. i.

of the Spirit in the organism, any more than such a "creative thought" caused the ape to evolve from the marsupials.

Our present age cannot speak about the facts of Nature as Jacob Boehme spoke of them. But there exists a point of view, even in this present day, which brings Jacob Boehme's way of regarding things near to a view of the world that takes account of modern natural science. There is no need to lose the Spirit, when one finds in Nature only the natural. Many do, indeed, believe to-day that one must needs lose oneself in a shallow and prosaic materialism, if one simply accepts the "facts" which natural science has discovered. I myself stand fully upon the ground of this same natural science. I have, through and through, the feeling that, in a view of Nature such as Ernst Haeckel's, only he can lose himself amid shallows who himself approaches it with a shallow thought-world. I feel something higher, more glorious, when I let the revelations of the "natural history of creation" work upon me, than when the supernatural miracle stories of the confessions of faith force themselves upon me. In no "holy book" do I know aught that unveils for me anything as lofty as the "sober" fact, that every human germ in the mother's womb repeats in brief, one after the other, those animal types which its animal ancestors have passed through. If only we fill our hearts with the glory of the facts that our senses behold, then we shall have little left over for "wonders" which do not lie in the course of Nature. If we experience the Spirit in ourselves, then we have no need of such in external Nature.

In my *Philosophy of Freedom*, (Berlin, 1894) I have described my view of the world, which has no thought of driving out the Spirit, because it beholds Nature as Darwin and Haeckel beheld her. A plant, an animal, gains nothing for me if I people it with souls of which my senses give me no information. I do not seek in the external world for a "deeper," "more soulful" being of things; nay, I do not even assume it, because I believe that the insight which shines forth for me in my inner being guards me against it. I believe that the things of the sense-world are, in fact, just as they present themselves to us, because I see that a right self-knowledge leads us to this: that in Nature we should seek nothing but natural processes. I seek no Spirit of God in Nature, because I believe that I perceive the nature of the human spirit in myself. I calmly admit my animal ancestry, because I believe myself to know that there, where these animal ancestors have their origin, no spirit of like

95

nature with soul can work. I can only agree with Ernst Haeckel when he prefers the "eternal rest of the grave" to an immortality such as is taught by some religions.* For I find a dishonouring of Spirit, an ugly sin against the Spirit, in the conception of a soul continuing to exist after the manner of a sensible being.

I hear a shrill discord when the scientific facts in Haeckel's presentation come up against the "piety" of the confessions of some of our contemporaries. But for me there rings out from confessions of faith, which give a discord with natural facts, naught of the spirit of the higher piety which I find in Jacob Boehme and Angelus Silesius. This higher piety stands far more in full harmony with the working of the natural. There lies no contradiction in the fact of saturating oneself with the knowledge of the most recent natural science, and at the same time treading the path which Jacob Boehme and Angelus Silesius have sought. He who enters on that path in the sense of those thinkers has no need to fear losing himself in a shallow materialism when he lets the secrets of Nature be laid before him by a "natural history of creation." Whoever has grasped my thoughts in this sense will understand with me in like manner the last saying of the *Cherubinean Wanderer*, with which also this book shall close: "Friend, it is even enough. In case thou more wilt read, go forth, and thyself become the book, thyself the reading."

---

* Cp. Haeckel's *Riddle of the Universe*.

∽

Copyright © 2025 by Alicia EDITIONS
Credits: www.canva.com; Alicia EDITIONS.
https://en.wikipedia.org/wiki/Theosophy#/media/File:Emb_logo.png
https://fr.wikipedia.org/wiki/Rudolf_Steiner#/media/Fichier:Rudolf_Steiner_signature.jpg
ISBN E-Book: 9782384555833
ISBN Paperback: 9782384555840
ISBN Hardcover: 9782384555857
All rights reserved.
No part of this book may be reproduced in any form or by any electronic or mechanical means, including information storage and retrieval systems, without written permission from the author, except for the use of brief quotations in a book review.